The American family has been in crisis for a number of years. Fifty percent of first marriages end in divorce, and sixty percent of second marriages do the same. So much for learning from our mistakes! Rev. Stenneth Powell has reached deep into the principles of God's Word and the application of his own life experience to produce a book that can transform the lives of many. May this be a compass to give direction to the family in the twenty-first century.

> Dr. James J. Seymour
> Professor of Religion, Saint Augustine's College
> Author, *Black History Through Blue Eyes: The Debt the World Owes to Africa*

*In **What to Do Before You Say "I Do"** Pastor Stenneth Powell strategically gives a detailed blueprint on how to make your marriage last. Be not deceived, this book is not only for married couples. This work is for the single, the married, the divorced, and the widowed. If you digest and assimilate the knowledge in this work, it will help you to make the decision about whether you should make such a big move now or whether you should wait. If you have suffered through marital crisis or seriously desire to avoid one, read this book! **What to Do Before You Say "I Do"** is a must read for anyone serious about loving and marrying.*

> Dr. Louis Greenup Jr. "The Marriage Doctor"
> Author, *Woman Love Your Body and Let Your Husband Love It Too* and *How to Stop the Other Woman From Stealing Your Husband*

Although many of the marriage classics of the past have been useful, the hour that we live in today demands a fresher, more relative approach to this vital topic. Powell has brought to the table such a contemporary flair in his new work. With its intentional humor and clear scholarship this work will help the teenager who is looking for love in all the wrong places as well as the mature who believe they've mastered this thing called love. A splendid work!

> Bishop LeRoy Bailey Jr., Senior Minister
> The First Cathedral, Bloomfield, Connecticut
> Author, *A Solid Foundation: Building Your Life From the Ground Up*

*The human heart is responsible for pumping and delivering blood throughout the body. Metaphorically the heart has been likened to the center of an important matter. Pastor Stenneth Powell in his work **What to Do Before You Say "I Do"** properly credits God as the One who delivers sustaining life to marriages and as the One whom all marriages should center around. He rightly suggests that a marriage without God has failed before it even starts. The gems offered in this work have the potential to permanently correct the failing averages. Critical reading!*
Judy Battles M.D., Cardiologist

This is an inspired book. It has the potential to cure millions of bad marriages and make millions of good marriages even better. Right on, Reverend Powell.
Elvin Feltner
Author, *Winning Is Everything*

WHAT TO DO

Ensuring a Strong

BEFORE

Foundation for Marriage

YOU SAY "I DO"

WHAT TO DO

Ensuring a Strong

BEFORE

Foundation for Marriage

YOU SAY "I DO"

STENNETH E. POWELL

What to Do Before You Say "I Do"

ISBN 1-880809-90-7

Printed in the United States of America
© 2003 by Stenneth E. Powell
Legacy Publishers International
1301 South Clinton Street
Denver, CO 80247
www.legacypublishersinternational.com

Cover design by: Nikki Braun

1 2 3 4 5 6 7 8 9 10 11 / 09 08 07 06 05 04 03

Dedication

I dedicate this book to my parents, both of whom are with Jesus now: the late Deacon Hubert Powell and Missionary Edith Powell.

You were the first example that I ever saw of marriage, and you still remain the finest.

Acknowledgments

To my wife—whom I have had the great fortune of being married to for the past twenty-two years. More than anything I want you to know how much I really love you and sincerely appreciate your allowing me to be used of God by sharing me with so many people within the body of Christ. Your love, support, understanding, and sacrifice will never go unnoticed.

Thank you, Stenneth Jr. and Joshua—a man could not ask for two more honorable sons. You both have grown to understand the meaning of sharing and sacrifice. I fully realize that it can be difficult to give up your time so selflessly to allow me the privilege of pastoring a church, evangelizing, and publishing the Word of God. From my heart, I love both of you more than you will ever know.

To one of my best friends, Pastor Aaron D. Lewis—thank you for your assistance in the overall development of the project.

To Abundant Life Christian Center—you are much like the strong lineman on a winning football team, faithfully working hard to make a quarterback look good. Also, over the years I have gleaned a tremendous amount of strength from Dr. James Dobson's teachings on his Focus on the Family broadcast. I credit many of the truths shared on the broadcasts as the gems that helped my marriage to become as strong as it has.

The first, the last, and the greatest—the Lord Jesus Christ. To Him be all the glory for the great and marvelous things He has done.

Contents

Foreword 11

Introduction 13

Chapter One   Building the Right Kind of Foundation 17

Chapter Two   The Grand Interview 33

Chapter Three   A Bride for Isaac 53

Chapter Four   The Proverbs 31 Woman 71

Chapter Five   A Mighty Man of Valor 89

Chapter Six   Where Are You Going in Life—And Who
                 Are You Taking With You? 103

Chapter Seven   Why Get Married Anyway? 115

Chapter Eight   Thou Shalt Not Burn—Understanding
                 Sex in Marriage 127

Chapter Nine   Five Things That Lead to the Death
                 of a Marriage 141

Chapter Ten   God's Marriage—The Model for Success . . . 149

About the Author 157

Foreword

The *New Lexicon Webster's Dictionary* of the English language defines marriage as such: "Marriage—The institution under which a man and a woman become legally united on a permanent basis." The main portion of this dictionary secured its copyright in 1972. Not only does it amaze me, but it also often saddens my heart to see just how far our society has strayed away, over the past three decades, from the standard of marriage that we all once upheld with great honor. In just thirty years, how have we allowed the rise of secular humanistic theory to dilute the values of family and marriage to the point that we can no longer properly identify what a marriage is from what it is not?

In *What to Do Before You Say "I Do,"* noted Pastor Stenneth Powell carefully examines not only the aforementioned question but also various questions concerning the rite of marriage that have gone unanswered for far too long. Far too many marriages are breaking up without a justifiable and scriptural cause. Unfortunately, far too few pastors and religious leaders have appropriately addressed this critical issue to help bring about a healthy resolution. Worse still, many of our distinguished clergy have in recent years fallen captive to the same spirit that has caused marital failure in others time and again. These are sure signs that the church of the Lord Jesus Christ as well as our nation are both in need of immediate help.

Like an NFL lineman, Powell tackles these heavy topics that seem too large for some and too swift for others to take down. In the same didactic fashion as he articulates the Word of God, Powell employs the method of teaching line by line and precept by

WHAT TO DO BEFORE YOU SAY "I DO"

precept. He deals with issues such as whether marriage is for you or not, sex in marriage, and why God believes that permanency is an achievable goal for every Christian married couple. Permanency should be the expectation for all marriages. That's the intended goal and the example given to us by the greatest lover of all time— the Lord Jesus Christ.

Despite the rise in divorces and a consistent pattern that has become a trend toward infidelity—sexually, emotionally, and mentally—there is still hope. Our hope does not lie within the negative example that is constantly projected through our airwaves or through loosely thought-out articles written in mainstream secular magazines. As with any problem in our land, if we make the quality decision to repent and seek the face of our living God, He promises to forgive us and put our lives back in perspective.

What to Do Before You Say "I Do" can be viewed as a blueprint to help lead you back to the way God intended for marital relationships to be. This book should be required reading for every couple both young and old who is contemplating marriage. No longer look to the world for carnal answers about this God-created institution called marriage. *What to Do Before You Say "I Do"* will help you to get back on track and stay there.

> *When I shut up heaven and there is no rain, or command the locusts to devour the land, or send pestilence among My people, if My people who are called by My name will humble themselves, and pray and seek My face, and turn from their wicked ways, then I will hear from heaven, and will forgive their sin and heal their land* (2 Chronicles 7:13–14).

Bishop Charles E. Blake
Senior Pastor, West Angeles Church of God in Christ
First Vice President of the Church of God in Christ, Inc.

Introduction

Truly, we live in an age when moral absolutes are vanishing as suddenly as the morning dew. It is becoming increasingly challenging to deal with topics that demand people live at a higher standard of moral excellence. Since the 1960s the topic of marriage has become one of those unfortunate "controversial" subjects. The rising rates of divorce and separation now have prompted many practitioners and so-called marital specialists—both within and without spiritual circles—into extensive study and exploration to understand why.

The disturbing element in the midst of all the intellectual flurry is this: Although more books, seminars, and counselors exist now than at any other time in history, *divorce statistics are still rising at alarming speeds*. Why? Perhaps the advice available today is not addressing the root cause of marital confusion. On the other hand, perhaps people are simply ignoring the knowledge provided. Either way, in many cases, couples just give up all hope of ever having a successful marriage.

If it were only couples who are not "born again" who are breaking up, then the whole issue would be understandable. However, the rate of marital failure within the church is nearly the same as in secular society. This problem has made itself comfortable within the church. Whatever happened to the idea of a lifelong marriage? Is it now just a fairy tale? Are the "until death do us part" vows no more than a script to be recited at a dress rehearsal in the vain hope that it will all come out right on the big wedding day? I certainly hope not.

I have read literally dozens of books that deal with the subjects of marriage, sex within marriage, and divorce and separation. Many were quite worthwhile reading. Others were no more than a memoir of the author's personal experiences in his or her own marriage. Learning from another person's experiences can at times be helpful in many areas. Yet, because marriage can be complex and since every situation is completely different from couple to couple, it is hard to find any man-made method that will work for every situation.

I did not write this book because I believe there are not enough works already written on the subject. Books on intimacy, marriage, and relationships flood the shelves at every bookstore. Rather, I wrote this book as a tool to be used, a tool that can help fix nonworking areas within any marriage, if the principles explained here are properly and consistently used.

To use any tool with effectiveness, you must know its purpose and its procedures. For instance, it would be silly to use a flat-head screwdriver to hammer a nail; that is not what the screwdriver was designed to do. Only when a screwdriver screws and unscrews is it working at its optimum performance.

Actually, using a tool without understanding both of these things—purpose and procedures—is potentially dangerous to you and to those around you. In the same way, you could take what you read here, and by using it improperly or with selfish motive, could seriously injure your spouse mentally, emotionally, and spiritually.

Since God is the one who designed marriage, it would make the best sense for anyone who is contemplating marriage to consult Him first on exactly how a marriage should function. Only He knows how to properly use the tools to build a marriage or to fix a seemingly irreparable marriage. After all, would you go to the Chevrolet dealer if you had an oil gasket leak in your late model Mercedes Benz? Of course you wouldn't.

In the same way, it should not make sense for you to entrust your marriage to the ear and counsel of someone who not only had no part in creating marriage but whose own marriage also may be experiencing a slow death. You should get advice only from the best. I cannot think of a more worthy model than God Himself. *What to Do Before You Say "I Do"* will explore not only exactly how God views marriage but also how He chose to deal with His bride Israel, even in her recurring unfaithfulness toward Him, as recorded in the Bible. Every promise in the Bible is based on this covenant (i.e., marriage) with His people.

This book is all about building your marriage—knowing which tools to use, how to use them, and when to use them. Some things come quickly in life; others come more slowly. Don't worry if this marriage process takes time. Usually those things that take time to build are of greater quality and last far longer than those things that are created in an instant. No matter what stage you are in, in this building process, if you will apply the truths in each chapter you will start the hopeful process of repairing, restoring, and enhancing your worthwhile union. If you're just beginning a relationship, then like a skyscraper or a cathedral, it will take much time and detailed attention to construct. However, after the building is up and everyone is allowed to view it, you will be thoroughly proud of what God has created within you. You will possess a godly pride—a feeling deep within that knows beyond any doubt that every second of time you and God invested were well worth it. I pray that as you read and study this book, each word will lead you into a greater dependency upon God for everything in your life.

"In the beginning God created the heavens and the earth" (Genesis 1:1). This verse is perhaps the greatest verse in all Scripture. As simple as it seems, it is yet very profound. In this verse God reveals Himself as the Creator, the builder of everything. Knowing this fact should put you at great ease. If He has the ability to create the universe, then working on your marriage is only a small task for Him. *"But Jesus looked at them and said, 'With men it is impossible, but not with God; for with God all things are possible'"* (Mark 10:27). All you have to do is believe.

Make the quality decision right now to no longer try to build your marriage your way. That leads only to frustration. Allow God to build your marriage, your house, and your family, and I guarantee you'll have a marriage that will last for a lifetime, the way God intended it.

> *Unless the Lord builds the house, they labor in vain who build it; unless the Lord guards the city, the watchman stays awake in vain* (Psalm 127:1).

Chapter One

Building the Right Kind of Foundation

Whoever comes to Me, and hears My sayings and does them, I will show you whom he is like: He is like a man building a house, who dug deep and laid the foundation on the rock. And when the flood arose, the stream beat vehemently against that house, and could not shake it, for it was founded on the rock (Luke 6:47–48).

Builders all over the world, regardless of the type of building they are in the process of erecting, know that the most important part of the process is the foundation. It also is *the beginning* of the process. The foundation is the starting point that ultimately determines how well the building will stand over a long period of time. With this in mind, then, the most important thing you can do *before* building a marriage is to lay a proper foundation. Think about it. What beliefs and ideologies do you hold about marriage now, while you are still single? What's your foundation for a marital relationship? If you are already married, what concepts did you hold about marriage when you said "I do"?

When the opportunity for love shows up at our door, we humans tend to follow our hearts more quickly than our heads. We don't take the time to really examine our foundations before framing the walls. We just toss up some boards, cut out a window and a door, and lay out the welcome mat. If we would take the time to deal with the many areas that need to be investigated long before we enter the marriage covenant with anyone, I firmly believe that the word *divorce* would disappear from our vocabulary. It literally would become a forgotten concept of the past, much like eight-track tapes and reel-to-reel recorders have.

> **If we would deal with the areas that need to be investigated *before* we enter marriage, the word *divorce* would disappear from our vocabulary.**

If you know what an eight-track tape or reel-to-reel recorder is, then you are showing your age! Most young people I meet have never even heard of them! Since the introduction of CDs, those older methods of recording and listening to music have become nearly extinct. Why can't divorce be outdated in the same way? I believe that if you will apply the principles in this book and if you will consistently ask the right questions at the very onset of a relationship, you will shut the door to divorce and lead the way to the new (yet old) concept of a life-lasting marriage.

GET YOUR PRIORITIES IN ORDER

One of the first areas in building a lasting marital relationship obviously should begin at the selection process. I'm sure you've heard the romantic phrase, "It was love at first sight." When I hear men and women make such claims, I know that their relationship is headed for disaster. Think about it. To choose a mate simply based on his or her looks is absurd thinking. Yet, it is one of the main reasons relationships fail. Believe me when I say that I am not trying to get you to look for the ugliest person you can possibly dig up and marry him! Looks *do* matter. However, *where* you place looks on your priority scale is very important.

Many things matter in life. Our goal should be to find out what matters most and pursue those things with all of our energy. (That alone is a principle that always leads to success.) Celebrated author and teacher Dr. Myles Munroe once said, "Never let what matters most suffer at the expense of what matters the least." Keeping your car washed, vacuumed clean, and occasionally buffed are things that matter. They help the overall appearance of your car. Such attention also bears a reflection on what type of person you are, whether detail-oriented or disorganized. However, if you had to make a choice between paying for your car to be professionally detailed or fixing your engine that just blew a head gasket, which would you choose?

If you have had practice at making mature decisions, you would choose to put the money into fixing your car's engine. Common sense would tell you that the looks of your car won't be seen and can't be appreciated if your car is not drivable. The buff and shine matter, but a working engine matters more.

A pastor friend of mine recently told me about a newly married couple he knows who needed a place to live. This husband and wife together had six children to feed, clothe, and shelter. They had two children together; the other four children were from previous relationships, two each. The couple desperately needed to purchase or rent a home so they could begin the process of building a stable and strong family.

The problem was both this man and woman had horrible credit. In most places, good credit is necessary in order to get a mortgage, car loan, or even a credit card. (It also is needed to help build a solid financial future with your spouse. I'll cover finances in greater detail later.) Out of a possible 900 points—900 being the more preferred credit rating—they both scored between 400 and 450. This score would not qualify them to buy anything, especially not a home valued at more than $100,000.

Miraculously, God caused this hopeful couple to qualify for a loan in which they had to put just three percent down as their down payment. In addition, this loan was written in a way so as to absorb all closing costs (which totaled more than $7,000) into the total loan. They would have to come up with only about $3,300 to close the loan, and they would become proud homeowners. For the next three months, this low-income couple struggled to save and raise the money needed to close. With hard work and a newfound discipline, they succeeded in saving the money. About two weeks prior to closing, they took all the money that they had just worked so hard to save and purchased furniture for each of the rooms in the house. Their action was in response to a

Super President's Day Sale television commercial from one of the local furniture retailers.

When it came time for them to close on the home, they could not produce any money. They'd spent every dime. Needless to say, their mortgage broker was irate. He had spent several hours working on this loan, pulling strings and asking for favors from the underwriting department, for this family who needed a home so desperately. The closing never happened. Yes, they lost the entire deal and are now renting an apartment in one of the worst crime-infested sections of the city. When the broker confronted them about their irrational decision, they both became indignant and defensive. Their explanation? They said it made no sense to them to buy a house without having furniture to put in it. Now they enjoy the feeling of owning new furniture and, because of their declining credit situation, may never own a home.

This story is true. Perhaps you can relate with it. This couple, because of ignorance and lack of vision, allowed the thing that mattered most (home ownership) to suffer greatly by the thing that mattered least (new furniture). There is a valuable lesson to learn from this story. You see, too often people behave this same way when choosing a mate. They tragically allow what matters most (character and integrity) to suffer for what matters least (looks and appearance).

What you see is not always what you get

Looks should be very low on your scale of priorities in choosing a lifelong partner. I've personally seen many relationships end tragically because the foundation was based simply on looks and not on character and commitment. Both men and women fall into this trap over and over again. Women, you spot a man who in your eyes is absolutely gorgeous. He notices that you are sending him signals that shout, "I'd be the happiest woman in the world if I had the chance to be with you." You give yourself away. Knowing that his looks are alluring enough to capture your heart, he proceeds to ask you for a date, for some of your precious, God-given time.

Without thinking twice you consent to spend a day with a total stranger. You never stop to think that this man could be a murderer, a rapist, a polygamist, or possibly even a child molester. Yet, without asking any probing questions, you give him your day only because he has a gorgeous bronze complexion and naturally curly hair. When you stop and think about it, this is absolutely foolish, yet it is the method by which many people begin relationships. Unfortunately, *most* relationships are based solely upon looks and physical attributes.

What most people fail to realize in their early years of dating is that regardless of how beautiful your spouse is now, his or her looks will change in time. When you first met your husband, he appeared to be a picture of health. He was in great athletic shape. He worked out playing basketball with the boys at least three times a week. On Mondays and Wednesdays he focused on upper body muscle training at the gym. Twenty years later he is a far cry from that toned look. He is totally out of shape. Well, actually he does have a shape—round. And he lacks the energy, vitality, and appearance that you were once so in love with.

How about her? Twenty years ago she looked like a picture-perfect princess. She had a perfectly thin waistline, made sure she ate the right foods (and not too much), and wore a seven dress size. You can still re-member how easily you carried her over the threshold into the villa in Santa Domingo on your honeymoon. Her skin was so soft, so healthy. Her flowing jet-black hair crowned her head. Her eyes sparkled like choice diamonds. Her figure was heart-stopping. Those days are now history. That was before she carried four children.

You marry the person on the inside, not the picture or even the illusion on the outside.

Now she would not dare to be caught shopping for clothes in the petite section. That's right—she has graduated to the plus sizes. Instead of watching everything she eats, she now eats everything she watches. Every day she uses a special lotion to combat her extremely dry skin condition. She gets her hair done every ten weeks to hide the gray. Things are no longer what they appeared to be at first.

The contrast that is so interesting is that although outward appearances have changed because of aging, the inward person has become wiser, stronger, and more attractive than ever. Understand that *this* is who you marry. You marry the person on the inside, not the picture or even the illusion on the outside. Yet, so many misinformed people persist in focusing on the outward rather than the inward characteristics of a person.

> *But the Lord said to Samuel, "Do not look at his appearance or at his physical stature, because I have refused him. For the Lord does not see as man sees; for man looks at the outward appearance, but the Lord looks at the heart"* (1 Samuel 16:7).

ALWAYS PUT GOD FIRST

Within the past two decades a recurring trend has crept into the church that not only has brought shame to Christians everywhere, but also has destroyed personal relationships with God. This shameful tradition is *intermarrying and interrelating between a person who professes to be a believer and one who does not*. At first this may not seem like a big deal to you. However, the deadly effects that this activity leaves on the soul are treacherous.

Unfortunately, many Christian believers do not have any problem with dating unbelievers. Many of our young Christian women wind up pregnant by men who have no interest, no love, and no respect for God. It would be unethical enough for unwed women to get pregnant by a church brother who also claims to be a believer, but intermingling with an unbeliever poses a far deeper problem. It is a great threat to the kingdom of God when believers intermarry with unbelievers.

When choosing a mate or a date, your very first requirement should always be that the person loves God. A believer should not even consider exchanging moments of intimacy on any level with an unbeliever. This area should never be compromised. I realize that many people consider this type of teaching to be old-fashioned and in some respects obsolete. Yet, this is the foundational teaching that builds strong marriages. Although we have strayed far from what God's Word instructs, we must return to His principles if our marriages are ever going to survive in this wicked and unfaithful generation.

It is a great threat to the kingdom of God when believers intermarry with unbelievers.

Can two walk together, unless they are agreed? (Amos 3:3)

The above verse in Amos 3 may help you to understand more clearly how *two people must be in spiritual agreement if their relationship is going to prosper.* Amos 3:1–2 opens with God issuing judgment on all twelve tribes of the children of Israel. He is punishing their sin, idolatry, and continued indifference toward Him. *"Hear this word that the Lord has spoken against you, O children of Israel, against the whole family which I brought up from the land of Egypt, saying: 'You only have I known of all the families of the earth; therefore I will punish you for all your iniquities.'"*

The word *known* mentioned here is a marriage word that means to have passionate sexual intercourse with, as a man would have with his wife. So the idea is that God placed a higher standard on Israel's behavior and attitude toward Him because they *knew* Him like no other people did. They were a special people, a chosen generation; therefore, they did not have the leeway to rebel as other nations appeared to have. Because of their intimate union with God, they were required to think like God, speak like God, and overall behave like God would behave.

Although they realized God's expectations of them, their behavior did not exemplify the character of God at all. Instead, they behaved like whores, lusting and going after other gods. Neither did the children of Israel show any real desire of even wanting to change their ways. This left God with no other choice than to punish His people for their lewd behavior. It is then God posed the question, *"Can two walk together, unless they are agreed?"*

In looking at this passage, one of the first things you need to know is that when God asks a question, it is not because He does not know the answer. He is God. He knows everything. Rather, God asks a question because He is trying to convey the answer to you or through you. God wanted the Israelites to know why He was going to punish them. God is a just God; He is not unfair.

I can remember getting a "whipping" when I was a little boy. I'm not exactly certain what this particular one was for since I got so many for doing different mischievous things. I remember my dad giving me a pep talk to prepare me for what was getting ready to happen. He would say stuff like, "I told you not to do that, yet you did it anyway. If you can't hear, then you're just going to have to feel. Didn't you hear me the first time?" My dad knew the answers; yet, he sort of needed to justify why he was going to punish me. I believe this is the same way God does things.

God wanted the Israelites to understand that He and they could no longer walk together because they were no longer in agreement. God's nature and theirs were different. God is a holy God. They were living unholy lives. "Your ways are totally opposite to Mine. How then can we have communion or fellowship with one another?" God was asking. The answer is obvious; they could not. Using this as a guideline, an unbeliever and a believer can never enter into the holy union of marriage and expect God's blessings or approval.

I've heard Christian women say, "I know he's not saved, but he treats me better than the Christian men do...I know he's not saved, but I believe he's going to get saved in time...I know he's not saved, but God still understands my heart...I know he's not saved, but God can make bad things become beautiful in time." That is just a short list of the many foolish things I hear said as a defense for crossing spiritual boundaries. The bottom line is, although these rebuttals all sound strong, they are all deceptive.

My background was entrenched in the power and demonstration of Pentecost. So I personally know quite well that God is a God who can turn situations around. Yet, at the same time, there are some situations in which God will withdraw Himself from your experience and leave you to fend for yourself (usually when you are disobeying). This crossing of spiritual boundaries is one of those areas. It is like drinking cyanide and saying, "God knows my heart and even though I should not have ingested this poisonous substance, He can still make my bad actions turn out all right." Surely the person who speaks like this is headed for a speedy death.

It is with this same irresponsible attitude that some Christians casually flirt with and in some cases sleep with the enemy. They know it's wrong, yet they still expect to return from their experience untainted. It won't happen. *Agreement is the place of power.* Where there is no agreement, there is no power. If you begin a relationship without having a common understanding and agreement on who God is and what He means to you, that union will not have the power to last.

You ask, "Well, what about the case in which a person gets saved after he or she was married, yet the spouse remains unrepentant?" In this situation, there was still agreement from the very beginning. They were both unsaved. That makes them compatible, coequal in a spiritual sense. Whoever receives the salvation of the Lord first, it becomes that person's responsibility to draw the other into a holy relationship with God through his or her faithful example. *"For the unbelieving husband is sanctified by the wife, and the unbelieving wife is sanctified by the husband; otherwise your children would be unclean, but now they are holy"* (1 Corinthians 7:14).

> If you begin a relationship without having a common understanding and agreement on who God is and what He means to you, that union will not have the power to last.

If you are a believer who is looking for a mate, unbelievers should not even be on your list. If a person confesses to be an unbeliever, then move on. If God isn't first in his or her life, and I mean really first, then the order is confused. It doesn't matter whether the person visited your church or not. If the person is not saved, then that candidate ought to automatically be disqualified. You should ask this very simple question of anyone whom you are contemplating sharing your time with—"Do you know Jesus personally?"

Whoever you ask that question of should be able to answer in a straightforward manner. If the person cannot answer that question without becoming evasive, he or she is not who God desires for you. It is as simple as that. God is first, then family. The family will always struggle when God is not in the place where He should never have been removed from, which is first. To start a relationship any other way only causes unnecessary grief and needless pain.

Even the wisest man missed it

> But King Solomon loved many foreign women, as well as the daughter of Pharaoh: women of the Moabites, Ammonites, Edomites, Sidonians, and Hittites—from the nations of whom the Lord had said to the children of Israel, "You shall not intermarry with them, nor they with you. Surely they will turn away your hearts after their gods." Solomon clung to these in love. And he had seven hundred wives, princesses, and three hundred concubines; and his wives turned away his heart. For it was so, when Solomon was old, that his wives turned his heart after other gods; and his heart was not loyal to the Lord his God, as was the heart of his father David (1 Kings 11:1–4).

In the past scholars and theologians used these verses to justify their belief that God opposes and curses anyone who marries a person outside of his or her race. Sadly, millions of people have been taught this lie and use it to substantiate their own racist attitudes and bigotry. However, God never opposed interracial marriage. Scripture tells us that God once punished Miriam for challenging her brother Moses' authority and judgment in this matter.

Moses, a Hebrew, married a black woman, and his sister Miriam seemed to have had a serious problem with his choice. *"Miriam and Aaron began to talk against Moses because of his Cushite wife, for he had married a Cushite"* (Numbers 12:1 NIV). *Cush* is a Hebrew word that literally means "burnt faced man." Hence a Cushite is a black man. God did not have a problem with Moses' wife or with the union. Moses had great favor in the sight of God; God spoke face-to-face with him. To His other prophets He revealed Himself in visions.

What God was and still is opposed to is His children marrying *strange* women. *Strange* in this context does not mean weird, peculiar, or odd. It has nothing to do with acting or behaving in a strange way. Here "strange" women are foreign women. Because they are from a foreign culture and land, they practice foreign cultures. They worship the gods and idols of their land. They practice the customs and rituals of their homeland.

The children of Israel were God's people; the land of Israel was and still is considered to be the Holy Land. Anyone who was not connected to Israel by birth or adoption was viewed as a foreigner to the land and to their spiritual values. So contrary to popular opinion, Solomon's problem was *not* that he had too many wives. Having more than one wife was not illicit but rather customary during the time that Solomon lived. In fact, as long as you could take care of the women whom you married, you were free to marry as many wives as you desired. For Solomon, it was kind of a status symbol, seeing as he was extremely wealthy.

What, then, was Solomon's problem? Solomon had a *strange women* problem. Sages of old considered Solomon to be one of the wisest men who ever lived. Yet, Solomon was not wise enough to outsmart the fiendish plan of the devil to turn him away from God. The main reason God strictly warned the Israelites not to have sexual relations with strange women was because the women would eventually turn their hearts away from God.

This is the same reason God warns believers today not to mingle with strange women and strange men. They don't share the same values concerning God as you do. They do not love your God. They don't really understand your commitment to going to church, studying your Bible, and listening to a preacher teach

God's Word. Often they are opposed to the idea that you serve God at all. However, they won't reveal their true feelings up front.

At first they may act as if it is totally fine and it doesn't bother them. "Don't worry, we can hook up later. Go to your Bible study, and I'll come pick you up after." It sounds like a good plan. Yet, deep down within them—perhaps unknowingly—is a diabolical plan from hell to ultimately destroy your relationship with God. You need to see them as being used by the enemy to destroy your relationship with God (which ultimately means that you, too, will be destroyed).

They'll start asking questions like, "Why do you have to go to church so much? Why should you have to give ten percent of all your money to the church? What is the church doing with all that money? Will God mind if you take a day or two off from church?" You still have ample time at this point to end this "ride" that never should have started. If you choose to let the ride continue, then they'll go from asking questions to making outright judgments. "You and the pastor must have something going on." (This is applicable to both sexes.) "They're brainwashing people down there. You're getting milked for all your money."

You have to make a decision. This decision is usually a life-and-death decision: "Do I continue to court the devil, or do I renew my vows to the Lord?" This is always an extremely difficult decision to make after you have given yourself to a strange person. I see it all the time. A young sister who is born again meets an unsaved brother and allows him to invite her into his world.

She starts going to the movies with him, going out to eat, and going to concerts at the park. She spends the kind of time with him that should be reserved only for someone with whom she is married to or soon to be married to. This exchange of time, conversation, emotions, and sometimes gifts all set the stage for this brother to win this sister's heart and soul.

Sister, if he was still a total stranger, he could not win your heart and soul. He would have no influence on you at all. But when you have allowed a stranger to become your intimate partner, you have made it very difficult for you to hear the voice of your first real love, Jesus Christ. Before you would never miss a service. You were always on time and ready to help in any area where there was a need. Now you have made it okay to have less devotion and dedication to God and your church. Now it is all right not to come to church at all, even though you are spending time with a stranger.

God knew that these strange women would mess with Solomon's mind if they were given the opportunity and enough time. Solomon would not turn from God just because he was with a strange woman only once. Rather, it became a habit that eventually became a part of his character. This new character was a direct reflection of the strange women who carved it out. This new character was one that directly opposed God. It did not happen overnight. It happened in time.

> For it was so, when Solomon was old, that his wives turned his heart after other gods; and his heart was not loyal to the Lord his God, as was the heart of his father David (1 Kings 11:4).

It is a sad situation when you are being deceived and not realize that it is happening. It is like the frog that jumped inside a kettle filled with cool water. As the kettle sat on a stove and *slowly* heated, that frog eventually got cooked but did not know it. You would think that the frog would have jumped out of the kettle as the water heated up. That would be logical, wouldn't it? However, when the world around you is changing at a slow pace, you often adapt to your surroundings. Like a chameleon, you change to fit in your environment. What is the solution? Stay away from strange (unsaved) men and women. In time they will turn your heart against God.

> "Same day leaf falls 'pon da water, leaf na rot. It tek time."
> (Jamaican proverb)

LOOK PAST THE FACE TO THE HEART

How will you know the right one?

> Beware of false prophets, who come to you in sheep's clothing, but inwardly they are ravenous wolves. You will know them by their fruits. Do men gather grapes from thornbushes or figs

from thistles? Even so, every good tree bears good fruit, but a bad tree bears bad fruit. A good tree cannot bear bad fruit, nor can a bad tree bear good fruit. Every tree that does not bear good fruit is cut down and thrown into the fire. Therefore by their fruits you will know them (Matthew 7:15–20).

When building the right kind of foundation for marriage, it is obvious that you need to put God first. You also should not use outward appearance as the sole reason for choosing your mate. And, under no circumstances should you link up with a non-believer if you are a believer. With all those in mind, you may be wondering, *How will I know who is the right one?*

Jesus gave a discourse, recorded in Matthew 7:15–20, in which He warned us not to look to outward appearances as a means of measuring the value of a person. He warned us that if we choose to focus on the outward appearance, we may be fooled into believing that a wolf is a sheep. Wolves often disguise themselves as sheep solely to destroy the sheep. For our purposes in this book, we will say an unassuming, naïve spouse-to-be may be the sheep a wolf is looking to prey upon.

He may come in a limousine, yet he doesn't really even own a car. Although he says he owns a condo on Grand Cayman and a summer home in Connecticut, he is really homeless. He talks a big talk. He has told you that he owns a computer support systems company, yet you discover later that he hasn't worked in years. She has told you that she's never had children. Months later you find out that she has three children who live with her mother and one who lives with the child's father.

Maybe you have experienced similar scenarios. How can you know who is for real and who is a fraud? Wolves give far too many details to verify. And many people are prone to give fictitious, superfluous stories anyhow. Again, Jesus gave the answer for how to know who and what a person really is. *"Therefore by their fruits you will know them."*

How will I know who is right or wrong for me? After I have made my choice, will I feel confident and strong, knowing that I have made the best possible selection? After all, there are many fish in the sea. How will I know if that person is the one whom God intended for me to share the rest of my life with?

"By their fruits you will know them." What is so powerful about this principle is that it can be used to produce longevity in business relationships, spiritual relationships, church relationships, friend-ships, and marital relationships. It is one of those principles you can use to usher success into many areas of your life.

What's so special about fruit, anyway? First, fruit grows over a period of time. So the implied reasoning is that it takes some time to know what this person will produce. Not only does fruit take time to produce, but it also produces in certain seasons. There are four seasons in any given year: winter, spring, summer, and fall. Each season represents an opportunity to observe whether or not a person will stand strong in different situations.

When I hear people say, "I just met this man last week, and God says that we are supposed to get married this week," I get concerned. Since fruit is seasonal, I believe that you need to ob-serve your potential lifelong partner for at least one year. One year represents all four seasons. Under most circumstances, you should be able to determine the quality of your potential mate in that pe-riod of time. In some cases it may require an even longer period of observation.

You should want to see that person under pressure. How does he handle hard times, depression, or unemployment? Does she get so discour-aged at circumstances that she resorts to drugs to ease the pain? Does he use one closed door as an opportunity to find or, better yet, create a new door? Hopefully your potential spouse does not become so comfortable with the idea of doing noth-ing that he or she never aspires to do any-thing worthwhile.

> **You need to observe your potential lifelong partner for at least one year.**

You will never know the answer to these questions if you don't allow enough time for evaluating the person. Is your man inclined to be verbally or physically abusive toward you? Does the woman of your interest have a faithful and committed heart? Or is she the kind of woman who always looks for the next best thing to come along?

Given the right amount of time, you will discover many things about a person. It's kind of funny that when looking for a home, most people will hire a licensed realtor to help them find the home of their dreams. Usually you have a list of things that you want in your new house. You may need a two-car garage for your vehicles. Maybe you want to have at least one and a half baths so that, just in case company comes over, you'll have enough.

Maybe you are looking for a certain amount of bedrooms, storage, a pantry, or even a den. Whatever your specifications are, you are pretty committed to getting exactly what you want. Your realtor tells you that it will take some time, maybe nine months to a year, to get what you are looking for. You tell your realtor, "Don't worry; I am not in a hurry. When I make this investment, I want it to be right. I don't want to settle for anything less than the best."

Interestingly enough, we all seem to have similar attitudes when purchasing things like homes, cars, yachts, jewelry (especially engagement rings), and vacations. We want to make sure that it's absolutely right. Unfortunately, when it comes to building a marriage, some people sell themselves far too short. Some settle for the scraps and leftovers rather than for an exquisite gourmet meal of a relationship only because they refuse to wait.

Countless tragedies could have been averted if the people had looked at the big picture and not given in to their flesh, which always desires immediate gratification. Friend, if you are considering marriage, yet have not had sufficient time to evaluate your potential partner, do the right thing and slow down the pace. It is better to call off plans than to call a divorce attorney to dissolve something that never should have been. Don't be hasty. Take your time and learn about your friend. By taking time beforehand to learn and observe, you will receive answers to many concerns and perhaps avoid wasting your most valued commodity—your time.

The plans of the diligent lead to profit as surely as haste leads to poverty (Proverbs 21:5 NIV).

Chapter Two

The Grand Interview

We all would agree, I think, that entering marriage is on a far greater level than buying a car or searching for a new house. We do so much legwork and research before we put a down payment on those purchases. How much more should we make sure that we know, without any doubt, that we are making the right choice for a spouse. Too often people get involved in a relationship with someone they do not know at all. That is so dangerous.

Long before you exchange covenant vows, there are many things you should do to ensure that you will have a strong and lasting marriage. Two of those are seeing if your potential spouse has a love for God as strongly as you do and waiting for several seasons to determine exactly what kind of fruit he or she bears. But, don't stop with those. There are many more things to consider other than someone's personal relationship with God. Please don't misunderstand me; your relationship with God is paramount as a base or starting point for any lasting relationship. However, just because your friend loves the things of God does not necessarily mean that the both of you have made a divine connection.

There are other things you need to know. There are some very crucial points that you need to discover up front, not ten years down the road. If you are contemplating spending your entire life with someone, I believe that he or she should be honest and transparent about any issues that may be still lurking in the shadows.

Marriages often dissolve because, months or years later, one spouse discovers something about the other that comes as a total surprise. It is perfectly natural to discover things about each other that you may not know at first—things such as personal likes and dislikes. That is healthy and normal. The whole concept of unfolding discovery is a vital aspect of marriage that adds enrichment and joy to the nuptial ride.

On the other hand, there are some things that can be quite destructive to discover after you've already exchanged your vows. These are the areas that we will cover next. Meanwhile, get in the habit of asking questions. You're not asking just to make conversation; rather, you're gathering information that can impact your life. You have a right to know some things in advance.

WORK—A NECESSARY COMPONENT

You have to have a J.O.B. if you wanna live with me

One area that I consistently see overlooked, yet should be so obvious, is the area of employment. Although both sexes share the problem of joblessness, I have seen men boycott this much-needed work experience far more than women have. You need to ask from the very start, "Do you have a job?" If the person does not, then you may need to reconsider choosing this person as your lifelong partner. Although it may sound somewhat facetious, work really is necessary in order to sustain human life. Everybody needs to do something productive on a regular basis, not just every now and then.

The very first gift God gave to mankind was work. He did not give man a woman first. Giving a woman to a man without him first having work is a natural disaster. He will never take care of her because he has not been disciplined to do so. Having a job gives a man the needed discipline to be a provider for his family. Work is preliminary training for the real world of rearing a family and sustaining a wife. It's like a marital boot camp. If a man cannot keep a job, then he disqualifies himself as a candidate for marriage.

This is the history of the heavens and the earth when they were created, in the day that the Lord God made the earth and the heavens, before any plant of the field was in the earth and before any herb of the field had grown. For the Lord God had not caused it to rain on the earth, and there was no man to till the ground (Genesis 2:4–5).

This Scripture says that *"the Lord God had not caused it to rain on the earth."* Rain, then as in now, always symbolizes abundance and productivity, which inevitably leads to wealth. Think about it—everything that exists, in some way or another, depends on rain. Without rain, farmers cannot grow the crops from which we get our food supply. There would be no such thing as a corporation because water must be used in order to produce most manufactured products.

Without rain there would be an insufficient supply of drinking water, which is vital to human existence. Baths and showers would be things of the past. (Whew!) Water is extremely important and we cannot live without it. Simply put, water is always needed. Yet in this Genesis passage, God had not caused any rain to fall because there was no man to cultivate the ground. In other words, God felt as though it would be a total waste of time to give rain, which produces an abundance of vegetation, because there was no one to harvest the crops.

Bringing increase has always been an area of expertise and pleasure for Jehovah Jireh—The Lord Who Provides. However, God will withhold such blessing if there is no one available who can receive it. Someone has to work the fields to reap the harvest. If people refuse to do the work then they will not have any more than they are willing to harvest. Jesus once said, *"The harvest truly is great, but the laborers are few; therefore pray the Lord of the harvest to send out laborers into His harvest"* (Luke 10:2).

If a man cannot keep a job, then he disqualifies himself as a candidate for marriage.

Can you imagine a shortage of working men during the time of Jesus' earthly ministry? Luke 10:2 confirmed that the laborers were few. The same situation exists today. Any civilized society has more than enough work. If you cannot find a job and you live in a capitalistic society, then you have the option of creating your own job. This leaves a nonworking man with no excuse not to work. There is much to be done.

Even if we are in the middle of the worst economic recession, there is still plenty of ways to earn an honest living. The economy should not dictate whether we have work or not, especially for the Christian believer. There *always* will be someone in need of your service and who will gladly exchange his money for your services. There are millions of dollars to be earned; there are billions of souls still to be won to God, yet Jesus sadly exclaimed, *"The laborers are few."* God is looking for people who will work.

Then the Lord God took the man and put him in the garden of Eden to tend and keep it (Genesis 2:15).

God put mankind in Eden so that he could work in the garden and keep it properly manicured. Long before a woman came into the man's life, he first had a romantic relationship with work. This romance with work is so needed before you become married. Brother, sister, hear me. A man must have a job. And the job he has should be one that he has some sort of track record with. It shouldn't be a job that he started last week.

He should be able to prove that he can keep a job over an extended period of time. Why is this important? For a man, a job is not merely a source of income or the proverbial breadwinner's position. It is far more than that. A job is a character definer. It is a barometer by which we can measure how a man will be able to handle pressure, how he deals with potential conflict, and whether or not he will remain faithful under varying circumstances.

If a man walks off a job because someone said something that he does not particularly care for, he will do the same thing in a marriage. It is a reality of life that not everyone sees things eye to eye. However, that does not justify severing needed relationships with your employer. Seeing eye to eye is not why you work for who you work for. You work for your employer to do the job that you are skilled to do. You give the company your skills, services, and expertise, and in exchange you get money.

It's that simple. The people whom you work with do not necessarily have to be your best friends. They do not have to even be cordial to you. You are not there for that. You are there to perform a service, usually within an eight-hour time frame each day. After that you are free to go home. So if the person you believe you love continues to makes excuses for why he gets fired or why she quits every job she has, you may need to look a little deeper into the person's character. As I said before, people's relationship with their job will reveal their character.

It is totally unrealistic for anyone to get fired from every job he or she has started. Every boss cannot be all bad. All employees are not out to get you. If you have been fired from the past five or six jobs that you started working, perhaps you should take a closer look *at you*. Ask yourself some questions. "Do I often come to work late? Do I have enthusiasm about my job, and does it show? Do I display the proper attitude and respect for people who are in authority? Am I disrespectful? Am I obnoxious?

"Are people usually glad when I am in their company? Am I a hard worker? Am I lazy? Will I work only if someone is monitoring my progress? Will I work with great diligence if no one monitors what I do? Do I learn quickly? Am I able to understand complex concepts? Am I dependable? Do I go above the call of my duties? Do I rarely meet the minimum requirements asked of me?" The list can go on and on. By asking yourself these types of questions and answering them honestly, you will be able to discover why you cannot keep a job.

> People's relationship with their job will reveal their character.

More than that, you will at least have a point of reference from which you can make major changes for the better. If you are in a state of denial, you will never change. However, realizing where you messed up and correcting your mistakes puts you right back on track. Don't be afraid to ask a potential spouse these questions—"Do you have a job? Do you enjoy working on your job? How long have you had this job?"

Sister, if you're desiring a husband, these telltale signs are gifts from God to you. If you sense this kind of inconsistency in a man's character as it relates to his work, marriage to him will only prove to become a greater tragedy. If he leaves his job because he refuses to listen to his employer's complaints, perhaps he will do the same thing when you voice your complaints about his behavior.

A WOMAN MUST WORK, TOO

Although I do not believe that a woman should be made to work a secular job, I feel she should work in some capacity. Now, I realize that women in today's society are functioning in roles that were considered to be unconventional only thirty years ago. Clearly times have changed, and we should welcome the change. Without change we cannot grow.

However, I am not advocating that women fight hard to find their niche in the business world. If a woman chooses to climb the corporate ladder, then I applaud her efforts and commend her. On the other hand, if a woman chooses to be a stay-at-home mom and work in the home to provide the infrastructure that builds strong families with strong values, then that is commendable also.

In our money-driven society, it seems as if we have lost a sense of value for the things that help to create healthy and safe communities. We tend to downplay and often diminish the high value of the woman who chooses to raise her children in the fear and counsel of the Lord. My mother was such a woman. I have fond memories of seeing my mother in the home fulfilling her responsibilities, making sure all my brothers and sisters were properly clothed and fed.

My beloved mother taught my siblings and me what it meant to have a relationship with God. We often heard Mom praying to God out loud, asking Him for His protection and guidance over us. She taught us by example the necessity of going to church every Sunday for Sunday school, Sunday morning worship, and Sunday night service. We went to Bible study every week and listened to my pastor, the late Bishop I.L. Jefferson, teach the Word of

God in a practical manner. In the summer we participated in vacation Bible school. We sang in the church choir.

Sometimes it seemed as if we lived at the church, we were there so much. However, through that example, I learned the value of faithfulness. To this day I can appreciate how much that lesson has helped me in my previous job at American Airlines, where I worked for twenty years. Mom's example of faithfulness also has helped me to understand the value of being a faithful husband, father, businessman, and shepherd to those I pastor. Her deposit in all of her children was invaluable.

When I was in grade school I clearly remember my mother being there for me whenever I had a problem in school. She never seemed to be too busy to minister to the needs of her six children. We all had a reverence for my mother and father that I rarely see among young people in today's busy "dollar chasing" culture. Regardless of the many things that my mother did, she put the job of raising her children at the top of the list of her lifelong priorities.

Is this a memoir about my mother? Not quite. What I am trying to convey is that a woman must work, just as a man is required to work. Although her function may be domestic in nature, it is work nonetheless. I also am trying to correct the disparaging way that many people look down on women who raise their children. Although it is worthy of merit to work for a Fortune 500 company, it is equally if not more important to raise the children unfortunately orphaned by their working-class parents.

Sad to say, the respectable job of raising children has been replaced with daycare centers and after-school programs. Nintendo, Gameboy, and XBox games are substituted for spending quality time with our children. At one time parents took the time to read to their children, helping them strengthen their phonetic and comprehension skills. Now we have Ebonics, an approved system of undermining the language skills so desperately needed to compete in today's society.

Few things are as exasperating as a lazy woman. Failure is inevitable in a marriage in which both parties are unwilling to contribute their part to making the marriage work. A quality man desires a quality woman. Just as much as most women dream of marrying an aggressive, "go getter" man, men also dream of marrying women who will complement them in every way.

And the Lord God said, "It is not good that man should be alone; I will make him a helper comparable to him" (Genesis 2:18).

Note that word *helper*. God's desire from the very beginning was that a woman should help her man. In what way should a wife help her husband? Simple—wherever a man lacks, then God has commissioned that wife to help. In other words, a wife helps her husband in his areas of weakness. Some men are great laborers yet do not have any discipline with balancing their checkbook. In this situation a woman should help her man have greater financial integrity by compensating in the area of his apparent failure. She is the one who should balance the checkbook!

We can look at this issue from another perspective as well. Perhaps your husband is an alcoholic or a substance abuser. Being his helper does not mean you become his enabler. You cannot feel sorry for him and just allow his deadly addiction to kill him. Rather, you are commissioned by God to figure out—with His help—how to minister to your husband in such a way that alcohol or drugs will no longer be appealing to him. Believe me, helping to restore a broken man is hard work. It is just as hard as working a nine-to-five job.

Perhaps your husband does not earn enough money to make ends meet. Maybe he is trying the best that he can, yet, because of circumstances (lack of education, high unemployment rates, sudden layoffs, and downsizing), he does not earn enough to meet the bare requirements. In this situation, a woman should help the man meet his financial needs. Now, I am not suggesting that she become the breadwinner and sole provider for the entire family. I am merely suggesting that she use common sense and recognize that she may have to work for a season until the husband gets financially readjusted.

You should help your husband meet his needs in whatever way you can. A woman should work hard to ensure that her husband always has a healthy image of Christ and His church through her example. Wherever the man is lacking spiritually, it is the woman's role to help lift that man back to his rightful place as a priest, prophet, and provider of his household.

I have heard men—both married and those contemplating marriage—complain about how lazy some women are. Many of them shared with me that their concept of the ideal woman is one who is actively working prior to getting married. In fact, many men have used "whether she works or not" as a measuring tool to determine if a female friend would qualify as a quality lifelong partner.

> **Marriage is hard work. If you happen to disdain the whole idea of working, then marriage is not for you.**

Lazy men and lazy women both are equally irritating and unproductive. And if this spirit of laziness is not dealt with and conquered before entering into marriage, it will surely lead to major problems down the road. Marriage is work, hard work. So if you happen to disdain the whole idea of working, then marriage is really not for you. You may want to seriously rethink the whole idea of marrying someone. Benefit from the wisdom of Solomon concerning the spirit of laziness:

> *As vinegar to the teeth and smoke to the eyes, so is the lazy man to those who send him* (Proverbs 10:26).

LOVE IS THE BOTTOM LINE

Why do you love me?

Of the many questions you must have answers to before you dare enter into a marriage covenant, one of the most important is this: Why do you love the person you are contemplating marrying? If you cannot come close to answering that question, then you should reconsider getting married, at least to that person. Answers such as, "I just love 'em," "I really don't know," and "Because he makes me feel good," are all unsatisfactory. And I don't think that it is unfair for you to pose that question to your potential spouse: "Why do you love me?" You really need to know.

One time a young sister, when given premarital counseling by her pastor, was asked, "What makes this man different from the past four guys you dated?" The pastor reminded this young lady that the four men whom she had dated within the past two years had all been engaged to marry her. She had seriously planned on marrying each guy she dated.

At first glance there were no particular criteria for her choices in a mate. Two of the guys she met in a nightclub. The other two she met sort of accidentally, one at the bus stop and the other while visiting her sick aunt at the hospital, where he happened to work. Although this sister professed to be a born-again believer, she still lacked the spiritual fruit needed to make quality decisions concerning who she should and should not allow into her life. The truth is that she, like many other people, was looking for someone to free her from the reality of her abusive past.

Sadly, her uncles and cousins had sexually molested her since she was six years old. When she was fifteen, a total stranger raped her. This cycle of abuse had a very destructive effect on her mind. She became increasingly incapable of making rational decisions about relationships. Eventually she began to view marriage as an opportunity to escape her old realities. She saw it as a way to enter the new and escape from the old, even if the new proved to be just as abusive. Three of her previous fiancés physically abused her. One of them actually raped her. However, she rationalized the whole ordeal by claiming that "rape is different if you know the person. It isn't really rape." All in all, the new abuse seemed like a fair exchange for marriage. Now she was looking at marrying candidate "number five." Her fiancé's past life, however, was just as much a wreck as hers was.

This young man had been married before. His first marriage ended within the first year. He claimed that he was too young when he decided to get married. "I wasn't informed; I hadn't seen the world," he said. Looking back, he now believes that the girl's parents kind of forced him to marry in the first place. A nineteen-year-old young man was just too young to get married, he thought. Now, at twenty-four years of age, he was at it again. Like a gambler, he was trying the "marriage game" once more.

So the pastor began the counseling session with the question, "What makes this man different than the past four?" She looked at her pastor as if he was asking a trick question. She pondered the question for a few moments. Then, with all sincerity she responded, "I really don't know. I can't answer that question right now." The pastor was disappointed by her answer, and he assured her that if he were to give his blessing over this marriage, she would have to properly answer that particular question.

Since this was the first time her fiancé officially met her pastor, she was quite embarrassed. Perhaps she (like many others) thought her pastor would join them together in holy matrimony without asking any probing questions. Pastors and spiritual leaders who marry young people without giving them the truth concerning marriage are only doing the unmindful couple a terrible disservice. Knowing within that this marriage would probably fail, the pastor suggested that this young sister and her fiancé continue to receive further counseling.

He also informed her that she must get a firmer understanding of the purpose of marriage, as well as to get to know this man whom she had known only for the past three months. He told her that perhaps a later wedding date would be a better decision for them. He felt that time would help to reveal to them whether they should pursue the relationship any further. Unfortunately, she did not heed her pastor's advice. She hired a ninety-eight-year-old pastor to marry them. Sadly, her marriage lasted a miserable three months. It ended in a horrible divorce.

"*Why do you love me?*" The answer should not be some coined cliché. But I do believe that you should have some response. Although such responses will vary from person to person, it should still be a solid one. The answer should not leave you doubting whether or not your potential mate really loves you.

Love is not based on emotion or feelings. Love is not a feeling. *Love is a choice.* Just as I can choose to love, so I can choose not to love. Why do I love my wife Beverly? It's not because I feel like loving her every day I get out of bed. And I am sure she does not always feel like loving me. No, we *choose* to love each other.

You see, feelings and emotions are much like a thermometer. It changes as the weather changes. If it is cold outside, then the temperature drops. If it heats up, then the temperature gradually increases.

Love is not a feeling. Love is a choice.

Love should not be like a thermometer. There are some days when I may offend my wife. Other days she may be prone to shut me out mentally (temporarily, that is). If my reason for loving her is based on things always going the way I believe they should go, then my marriage would have self-destructed many years ago.

I love my wife for the same reason you should love your spouse—you choose to. Since love is based on the will (on your ability to choose) and not on emotions, your love should last a lifetime. A decision is a stronger and firmer foundation for your love than emotions. Emotions come and go. They are like a seesaw, always going up and down. Like the tide, they ebb and flow. But, when you make the quality decision to love, that decision cuts off any other possible scenarios from taking place.

God Himself made one of the greatest choices ever—He chose to love the world. I am convinced that He did not feel pleasure about offering His only Son as a blood sacrifice to prove His love to us. What good father would want to witness the death of his son? However, God's love was firmly rooted in choice, not feeling. If His actions were based on feelings, He may have changed His mind.

But God could not change; He had already made the choice. In the same way, once you have made the choice to love, it is extremely difficult to look backward. So ask your love-to-be, "Why do you love me?" I am certain that you will receive many different answers at first. Just make sure that this one follows all the answers that come before: *I choose to love you.*

> For God so loved the world that He gave His only begotten Son, that whoever believes in Him should not perish but have everlasting life (John 3:16).

For better or worse

Why is it so important for you to know why your spouse loves you? There comes a time in every person's life when love will be put to its greatest test. It is vital for you to know that your loved one will be there for you in the worst of times. Let's face it; anyone can be there for you when things are going well. But it takes a totally different kind of person to be there for you when the future is bleaker than a cold winter morning.

All we have to do is turn on the evening news to know that tragedies happen every day. The reality is that tragedies are inevitable. Tragedy will come either by firsthand experience or vicariously. No one gets through life without experiencing some type of tragedy. Although we do not welcome or anticipate it, we must be ready with a plan in place for how to deal with it.

Right now, let's troubleshoot the cracks in a marriage. First, ask straightforward questions. Deal with the possibilities now, not later. You want to hear heartfelt responses that will tell you whether the person will really be with you if it actually came down to a "for better or for worse" type of situation. It's easy to declare loyalty and fidelity when everything is flowing smoothly and all is well. But will that person keep his or her commitment to you whom he or she claims to love so dearly if you no longer fit the ideal description of a spouse? (You should pursue marriage only if he or she can answer "yes" to that question.)

Life is full of "what ifs." Although we do not intentionally expect the worst to happen, it is often good practice to sort of brainstorm some "what ifs" ahead of time, just to see what kind of response you will receive. Of course, I realize that the truest response comes out only when an actual tragedy happens. However, by confronting these possibilities head-on you may discover things about your loved one that you never would have believed. In fact, you will discover the individual's true character, not the person he or she has been portraying.

Look at it from your perspective. What will *you* do if your spouse is diagnosed with terminal cancer and immediately has to undergo extensive chemotherapy treatments? Suppose your spouse's gorgeous hair is one of the main reasons you are attracted to him or her. How will you adjust knowing that all that hair will be lost? Will you still remain faithful? Will your spouse still be attractive in your eyes?

Or will you now suddenly have a total change of heart concerning your love, loyalty, and commitment to your mate? I'm sure that these are not your everyday list of questions concerning marriage. Yet, they serve a real and valid purpose. Your genuine response to these questions will determine if you actually are ready for this lifelong journey of discovery called marriage.

What if you receive a disturbing call from the hospital informing you that your spouse has been in a terrible automobile accident? The other driver and the passengers traveling with him all instantly died when the cars impacted upon one another. However, your spouse has miraculously survived the collision. The doctor, the paramedics, and the recording police officer all agree that your spouse is most fortunate to be alive and in all reality should be dead.

Naturally your response will be one of great gratitude to God for preserving the life of your beloved one. However, the doctor feels compelled to share a bit more information with you. He tells you that your spouse was trapped underneath the steering wheel in an awkward fetal-like position while both legs were crushed up against the side of the drive shaft. Your loved one was in this position for nearly forty-five minutes before the rescue crew was able to get him or her out.

Unfortunately, during that time all the blood circulation was cut off to both legs, causing irreparable nerve, muscle, and tissue damage. The doctor continues that both legs will be useless, and that he has no other choice than to amputate both legs from the thigh area. Perhaps your spouse's legs were an attractive factor to you when you were dating. Now those legs are gone. Is it possible that your love for your spouse might diminish slightly, or do you feel the same level of commitment to your spouse as you did prior to the accident? Will you leave your mate? Will you fight for him or her? How long will you take care of your spouse?

I realize that I have used some very drastic illustrations to communicate my point, although these situations do happen in life. However, it could be something as trivial as your spouse gaining a little weight. That may sound a bit silly, but it is reality. Married couples today separate over the most foolish concerns. Too often it is over image.

In our image-driven society there is a perceived impression of what is beautiful and what is not. The preponderance of Hollywood on our culture often forces us to think and act like the movies and its stars. There is a perceived value of a person who is fat versus a person who is thin. Although we hate to admit it, many of us have succumbed to this low-thinking mentality also. Movies such as *Shallow Hal* crystallize the message of how society not only views people who are overweight but also discriminates against them in many areas of life.

Shallow Hal is a comedy and is meant to entertain the viewers, holding them in hysterical laughter. However, after the laughing has ceased the realistic individual is forced to admit that the satire has more truth to it than most of us are willing to acknowledge. Dating and even common social exchange is often enhanced and encouraged when the one with whom we spend our time mirrors society's overall image of "in shape" beauty. Thus the clause "for better or for worse" has a different meaning and value depending on the persons involved. Whatever the situation, tragedy, or change that may come into your life, will your spouse still be there for you? Will you be there for him or her?

I hope you never have to experience such great sorrows in order to realize the depth of your commitment. I pray that you never have to experience tragedy such as I have described. I pray that your life will be one of joy and happiness. I described such scenarios in order to make you think. I want you to give the proper heartfelt response to your lifetime vows.

If you choose to love as God has chosen to, then you and your marriage partner will stick together through all of life's storms. Marriage is still a far greater institution than most people in our modern culture realize. My prayer is that you will begin to respect this institution and highly revere it by not entering into it lightly as so many millions do.

> *The Pharisees also came to Him, testing Him, and saying to Him, "Is it lawful for a man to divorce his wife for just any reason?" And He answered and said to them, "Have you not read that He who made them at the beginning 'made them male and female,' and said, 'For this reason a man shall leave his father and mother and be joined to his wife, and the two shall become one flesh'? So then, they are no longer two but one flesh. Therefore what God has joined together, let not man separate"* (Matthew 19:3–6).

SOME THINGS MUST DIE

Over the years, I have noticed that many people who are getting married at times seem reluctant to give up old acquaintances. Yes, it is hard to do. Nevertheless, some things have to go, and old relationships are included in that list. When I as a pastor am conducting premarital counseling, I always ask if there are any past relationships either candidate has not ended yet.

Often the couple is taken by surprise by the question. Usually one or both don't want their partner to know that there is an old flame that might be rekindled. Let me ask you: Why is it necessary for you to keep the cell phone number of your past male or lady friend? Why do you need his beeper number? Is it necessary for you to still keep in contact with her? I know you are only doing "business matters" with the person, right? Wrong!

When you enter a marital union, it's a new relationship that must not have old shadows cast over it. There are many things that have to die in order to bring life to newlyweds, and among them are old past friendships, both sexual and platonic. You must cut those relationships off. Now I realize how important friendship is. I fully understand how important strong friendships can be. Good friendships can add an enormous amount of strength to your life.

But, when you are ready to marry your spouse, he or she should become your ultimate friend. If your fiancé or fiancée is not your best friend, then maybe you should consider marrying your best friend instead (of the opposite sex, of course!). Simply put, life as it used to be can no longer be if you are going to have a successful marriage.

This goes even for the guys who insist on hanging out late shooting pool, playing basketball, or watching Monday night football with their buddies. There is nothing inherently wrong with any of those activities. But, when you get married, your time should be reserved for your partner. You should always be available to serve and please each other. Your desire should be toward each other. And you should prefer your spouse above yourself. When the guys insist on going out every other night, their desire could cause you to neglect your wife, who just wants to spend time with her beloved man.

> **If your fiancé or fiancée is not your best friend, then maybe you should consider marrying your best friend instead.**

Nevertheless let each one of you in particular so love his own wife as himself, and let the wife see that she respects her husband (Ephesians 5:33).

When entering into the marriage covenant, your commitment to each other should be so strong that it overrides all other family attachments, mental and emotional attachments, etc. Even your own mother and father have to take second place when it comes to your spouse. Does that mean God wants us to devalue our relationship toward our parents? No. God only wants us to recognize the prioritized divine order for our marriage. Our spouse comes first.

You may say, "But my mother and I are tight. We are super close, and when he marries me he is marrying the whole package, mother and all." That may sound commendable, but it is totally unbiblical. It is also one of the many reasons marriages dissolve. (I'll talk more about the various reasons marriages dissolve in Chapter Nine, "Five Things That Lead to the Death of a Marriage.") God's Word addresses this specific point.

> *And Adam said: "This is now bone of my bones and flesh of my flesh; she shall be called Woman, because she was taken out of Man." Therefore a man shall leave his father and mother and be joined to his wife, and they shall become one flesh* (Genesis 2:23–24).

Even if you have to sever family ties for the sake of your marriage, you must put your spouse first. Why? The *future* of your marriage supersedes any *past* connections. For now realize that you must become healthily absorbed in each other in order to get your marriage off to a good start. There will come a time in the future when healthy friendships may be reactivated.

The future of your marriage supersedes any past connections.

There are so many things to learn about one another during the infancy of your marriage that other people may only distract you from the more important issue: your marriage. So whatever it takes, be willing to sever those things that need to be severed. If you cannot make yourself do this, then you may want to reconsider marriage.

I'M ALREADY MARRIED. AM I DOOMED?

Perhaps you are already married. "How can this information benefit me?" you wonder. You never asked the right questions when you got married, and now you are suffering the consequences of your neglect.

You followed your emotions rather than smart thinking, and now you are experiencing another emotion: grief. Not to worry. If you are already married, understanding the root causes of the problems in your relationship can help you identify strategies for alleviating the problem.

As long as there is life there is hope. For instance, people may do all the right things to prevent the possibility of getting cancer. They eat the proper cancer-fighting foods, exercise regularly, and oxygenate their blood through proper breathing and daily water intake. Unfortunately, due to the increase of toxins and pollutants in our air and drinking water, even people who follow all the right instructions may still get cancer.

What these preventative measures do is drastically *reduce* the possibility of getting cancer. Prevention is key to longevity. Of course, you can always do those things that increase the possibility of getting cancer. Horrible habits such as smoking cigarettes and abusing alcohol will position you in the top place for receiving lung and liver cancer.

Nevertheless, just because you got cancer does not mean that you are doomed to death. There are skilled medical physicians who can treat your condition, either to help you live with it or eliminate the whole thing. As long as you are willing to do what is prescribed and get involved with your healing process, you will have a great chance of surviving.

In the same way, by pinpointing the root causes that began the problems in your marriage you will be able to uproot the problem and usher in the cure. Just knowing why things happen can itself be a great relief for the searching soul. At least when you know the reason you can deal with it. Denial is an overpopulated state.

Usually people move into a state of denial because they are trying to escape the realities of the state they are living in now. It is more comfortable to avoid the real reasons for their suffering than to confront it truthfully. You see, everything in life really does happen for a reason. And when you know the "why," you can get so much further ahead and possibly get back on the road to nuptial recovery. So whether you are contemplating marriage or are already married, take heart. You can succeed in having a lasting marriage.

Chapter Three

A Bride for Isaac

One of the greatest love stories in the Bible is the marriage of Isaac and Rebekah in Genesis 24. Although our dating methods are a far cry from the arranged marriages of old, there is much that can be learned from the parents' high standards in choosing a mate for their children.

Abraham was a wealthy man, and his son Isaac was set to inherit a great responsibility. Abraham also knew his son Isaac was chosen by God. So he was very particular in what he looked for in a potential wife for Isaac. First, the woman had to possess a certain kind of character. She had to be willing to be submissive to authority. Her family lineage had to meet a certain standard of excellence. Also, she had to be blessed with gracious outward beauty. There was kind of an unspoken checklist of which all the points needed to be satisfied in order to make her the bride of choice. After all, much had been invested in Abraham's son Isaac throughout the years.

Just any woman would not do. She could not be from just any tribe or nation. This woman had to be a special woman, one who was spiritually compatible. Since Isaac would be the progenitor of the Messiah Himself, Abraham had to make sure that this woman would not be a person who would potentially alter the destiny of a nation.

When you truly understand some of the traits that Abraham was looking for, you can add those characteristics into your process of finding a spouse. If you are already married, then you can use his high standards as a measurement for where you and your spouse should be spiritually, emotionally, and financially.

THE TRUSTWORTHY SERVANT

So Abraham said to the oldest servant of his house, who ruled over all that he had, "Please, put your hand under my thigh, and I will make you swear by the Lord, the God of heaven and the God of the earth, that you will not take a wife for my son from the daughters of the Canaanites, among whom I dwell; but you shall go to my country and to my family, and take a wife for my son Isaac" (Genesis 24:2–4).

The first thing to recognize is *whom* Abraham chose to find a wife for his son. Because marriage was such a highly valued institution, Abraham had to make sure that the one he sent to find a wife for his son was trustworthy. Imagine the disaster if Abraham had sent a servant who held a secret jealousy against him and his family heritage. Such a servant probably would have purposely set out to find the worst choice for a wife simply to disturb the harmony within his master's family line.

Just so that you will see how important this servant was to Abraham's family, I want to point out three characteristics that distinguished this servant from the others. First, he was *Abraham's* servant. He was the one who personally cared for and served his master Abraham. He knew how to take orders from authority. Much like the centurion who asked Jesus to heal his servant (as recorded in Matthew 8:5–13), Abraham's servant was qualified to give commands to others since he was a man who understood how to submit to another man.

Don't overlook this trait. We live in a society in which men have a very difficult time submitting to another man. Men often do not want to listen to what another man has to say. They think, *I'm a man just like he's a man. He puts his pants on just like I put my pants on. Why should I listen to him? I don't know what he's doing. I am my own man. I'm a grown man just like he is, so why should I care what he has to say?* Statements like these are common among men who do not want to submit.

Because of this anti-submissive attitude, many men choose to defy all authority. Their lack of submission teaches them to disrespect authority. Many men spending hard time in prison are there because of rebellion against authority figures. Now they are forced to submit to the rules and regulations of their warden. If the truth were told, every man has to submit to someone at some time in his life. *Submission* is not a bad word; nor is it intended to be bondage, as many have falsely believed. Submission—in a biblical context—frees you. It frees you to live profitably within our society and it frees you from the judgment associated with rebelling against authority.

> *Let every soul be subject to the governing authorities. For there is no authority except from God, and the authorities that exist are appointed by God. Therefore whoever resists the authority resists the ordinance of God, and those who resist will bring judgment on themselves* (Romans 13:1–2).

The second distinguishing characteristic of this servant is that he was an elderly man. He was older than most of the other servants in this household. Obviously this man had served in Abraham's house since his younger years and had built a solid reputation of being loyal, dependable, and trustworthy. During biblical times, age, when combined with giftedness, was often considered to be an indication of trustworthiness. When servants spent decades with their masters, their long tenures proved that their commitment was entrenched in their love for the one they served and his family.

Third, this man had proven so faithful over the years that he was entrusted to rule and govern everything that Abraham owned.

Common sense and good rational judgment will tell you not to put all of your earthly possessions in the hands of a stranger. Even if you have known someone for a long time, just knowing that person does not qualify him or her to have control over your possessions. It will take much more than that for you to entrust your goods to someone. You would give another person such an awesome responsibility only if you trusted that person with your very own life. This was the kind of person whom Abraham needed and chose to find Isaac a mate.

Scholars believe that this servant was Eliezer of Damascus according to Genesis 15:2, where Eliezer was referred to as the heir of Abraham's house. If this servant actually was Eliezer, then he had stewardship over Abraham's house fifty-four years before Ishmael, Abraham's first son, was born.

When Abraham gave this servant his instructions, he made this servant take an oath, which in that time was very serious business. If your oath was not carried through, you would be put to death.

> *Please, put your hand under my thigh, and I will make you swear by the Lord, the God of heaven and the God of the earth.*

The phrase "under my thigh" is significant. The thigh was considered to be the seat of generative power and the region of sacramental consecration, and to put the hand under the thigh was to acknowledge and pledge obedience to the man who required the oath. The seat of generative power would more clearly be understood as the testicles, which are responsible for secreting sperm. Sperm represents the very beginning of all human life.

Either way, Abraham was conveying this message: "If you break this agreement, not only will you have lied to God Almighty, but you also will have disrespected the generations that shall come from my loins." There is no possible way that a friend, a brother, or a genuine servant would ever cross his master this way. Abraham knew very well that his servant would complete the task. Abraham had found his man.

ISAAC—THE GOLDEN CHILD

I believe that every Christian should view him or herself as a child of promise—a golden child, if you will. Although Isaac was perhaps the most popular of Abraham's sons, he was not an only child. Abraham had eight sons in all. One was by a black Egyptian woman named Hagar. Six were by Keturah, his concubine. With his wife Sarah he had one child, Isaac.

Abraham was most concerned about Isaac, the son from his marriage, because he was the one who would inherit his wealth and become the main testator of the covenant of God. When it came down to it, Ishmael could have married whomever he wanted to marry. The six sons of Keturah could have married anyone they wanted to marry. Not Isaac. Isaac was a child of promise who had a godly purpose on his life. He could not marry just anyone; he had to have the right one. *When you are caught up in the purposes of God, your marriage and the person you marry are critical.*

I am often saddened when I witness young people—both male and female—throw their lives down the drain when they consciously choose to marry or cohabit with total losers. How can someone who has a great future and clear-cut goals spend time with someone who does not? I have seen lovely young women with earned degrees and high-paying jobs associate themselves with men who refuse to work at all.

Other women knowingly continue in a relationship with a person who is a substance abuser in the hopes that someday that man will suddenly change for the better. Accept this as truth: People just don't change for the better. No one goes to bed a blunder and wakes up a wonder. It just doesn't happen like that. Without the intervention of God's power, people rarely make changes that last. Only God can change a person's heart.

When you are caught up in the purposes of God, your marriage and the person you marry are critical.

Know that everybody with two legs does not necessarily qualify as your lifelong partner. You must see yourself as being someone special. And because you are special, it should be imperative for you to find that special partner to grow with. Just as a tree grows only in the optimal conditions for its sustenance, two people must have compatible characteristics that will ensure a lifetime of relational success.

If you were to uproot a tropical palm tree growing alongside the ocean at Daytona Beach, Florida, and plant it in the city of Hartford, Connecticut, where I grew up, it would surely die during the winter season. It doesn't matter how fertilized the soil may be; Connecticut ground is not a conducive factor for sustaining the life of palm trees. In the same manner, "he" or "she" may be beautiful on the outside, but it is what is on the inside that will determine whether or not the person is right for you.

No matter how we try to force the palm tree to stay in Connecticut, in a very short time it will surely die. Its growth and development only happen when it is in its right surroundings. In the same way, when you are with certain people, they can literally destroy your life because you have not been ordained by God to be with them. You are forcing the relationship. And although you have several telltale signs that your relationship is unfruitful, you continue to persist. Eventually, like the palm tree, your relationship will die.

When that happens, you will go through the rest of your life never being able to successfully hide the effects of your impediment. You will continually suffer from the aftermath of an ungodly relationship that left you crippled. This was a situation Abraham could not tolerate for his son. Isaac was not just any child; he was a child of promise. Through his loins the entire universe would come to know the Messiah. So only a certain type of woman would do for his mate. She would have to be sensitive to the spiritual realm. She would have to be someone who had a reverential fear for God. She also had to be someone with the right attitude toward money. For besides his spiritual endowment, Isaac also was the primary benefactor of his father Abraham's estate.

Abram was very rich in livestock, in silver, and in gold...Lot also, who went with Abram, had flocks and herds and tents. Now the land was not able to support them, that they might dwell together, for their possessions were so great that they could not dwell together (Genesis 13:2,5–6).

The Bible says that Abraham was not just rich, but *very rich*. In fact, he had so many possessions that he could not live comfortably with his nephew Lot because they got overcrowded. Can you imagine just how rich Abraham was? Do you know anyone who has been cited by the local zoning commission because he owned too many wealthy possessions? Abraham's possessions were very great. The Lord had prospered the hand of Abraham with not only a spiritual endowment but also an endowment of financial wealth.

There is a type of woman who will squander every single dime that her man has. She will neither save his money nor practice frugality. Everything that she sees, she wants to buy. She never considers tomorrow; she only thinks about today. In every way she proves to be an unwise woman because she does not understand the laws of reciprocity or how to multiply what is given to her.

This kind of woman is not the kind of wife that Isaac needed. Actually, this is not the type of woman that any good man would need. Even if you don't have great possessions right now, yet you believe God will increase your net worth, you must be very cautious about whom you connect with. Remember this phrase, which applies to both male and females: "Not just anyone will do." You must accept this motto as your guide for marriage. "Not just anyone will do."

Marriage is the only institution on this earth that God expects you to preserve until you die. You can study one semester at the University of North Carolina, transfer to Duke University, then to Shaw University, and then graduate from Morehouse College. No one would think that it was that strange. They would probably conclude that you absolutely love college life. With marriage, however, you cannot just choose to casually transfer from one agreement to another.

If you flit from marriage to marriage, after a while people will begin to conclude

> **You must accept this motto as your guide for marriage: "Not just anyone will do."**

that you suffer from major mental and emotional problems since your marriages are so unstable. Therefore, you must carefully consider who will be your lifelong partner. I mean, you should examine *every facet*. Abraham had so much invested in his son Isaac that he could not let his investment be destroyed.

You, too, should have the same attitude as Abraham had concerning Isaac. After all, your parents have invested years and years of quality instruction, discipline, finances, and loving care on you. Should just anyone be able to enter your life? Think about your future children. Do you want just anyone to enter your children's lives? What is your investment in them worth to you?

If you purchased a brand-new Rolls Royce Corniche convertible, would you be eager to give the keys to your fourteen-year-old to take it for a spin? I think not. Why? You probably just invested more than $285,000 of your money into it. The average fourteen-year-old does not know how to perceive that amount of invested value.

Quite innocently yet ignorantly the teenager would pick up three or four of his closest friends to take them out for a joyride. Being behind the wheel of such a highly visible automobile, he may feel the need to drive well beyond the posted speed limit. Not only would he be endangering the lives of those ecstatic passengers, but he also would be increasing the possibility of totally destroying his father's car.

Considering the high investment put into the vehicle, it would make far greater sense to entrust the car to a skilled driver, not a novice. In the same manner, you should view your life as one that people have the privilege of depositing into. To allow just anyone to enter your life would be as reckless as allowing a fourteen-year-old behind the wheel of a Rolls Royce.

Besides, in some ways such reckless choices would discredit the good things that people have deposited in your life over the years. It would suggest that you did not value the lessons, instruction, education, time, and finances they gave you. So don't choose just anyone as your mate. Your marriage will never be successful until your spouse genuinely understands your value and worth.

Remember, you are a child of promise. You have a destiny waiting to manifest. God has deposited so much in you, you cannot allow someone to deter you from your journey. But it is up to you to set the high standards that must be followed for anyone to participate in your life.

Your marriage will never be successful until your spouse genuinely understands your value and worth.

If you want an audience with a king or queen, you must first follow protocol. If you do not follow protocol, then your request will more than likely be denied. Gold never mixes well with brass, or even silver. Connect with the soul mate God intended you to be with. And make sure that he or she is golden too, just like you.

REBEKAH—WILLING TO FOLLOW A LEADER

We live in a society in which strong leadership has almost seemed to vanish over the past few decades. Again and again we try to redefine and distinguish what a leader is from what a leader is not. In the process of trying to find where our leaders are, some people have lost all hope of ever discovering genuine leadership.

Women are among those who have lost that hope. The fear of never finding a leader has caused many women to settle for far less than they should in a husband. They have compromised their convictions and high standards only to accommodate the constant failures within the men whom they chose to deal with. They have also compromised their convictions because, deep within, they really don't believe they will ever have a man who exemplifies true leadership ability. Finding a true leader for a husband has become sheer fantasy for many women.

Therein lies a great problem. The problem is that if men ever expect their female counterparts to follow them anywhere, then they must first know for sure where they themselves are going. In most cases, many modern men have no idea where they are going in life. Worse yet, they have no idea where they are going *spiritually.*

If a man does not have direction himself, then he cannot provide direction for anyone else, especially a family. So one of the qualifications for a good husband is that he first demonstrate a keen spiritual awareness and a solid ability to lead himself toward greatness. This is of great importance. No one can take you where he has not been.

One of the qualifications for a good husband is that he first demonstrate a keen spiritual awareness and a solid ability to lead himself toward greatness.

Unfortunately, in many cases relationships led by misguided men end up nowhere. If the man has not been anywhere, then how can he take you anywhere? Obviously he cannot. When traveling life's journey, you want a leader in the spiritual, mental, emotional, and financial realms.

It is interesting to note that Abraham's servant asked a very intriguing question. *"And the servant said to him, 'Perhaps the woman will not be willing to follow me to this land. Must I take your son back to the land from which you came?'"* (Genesis 24:5) What if the woman will not follow? This question was extremely pertinent because if the woman refused to follow, then it would have forced Isaac into a follower's mode rather than the leadership role that God predestined for him.

Suppose the bride-to-be insisted on Isaac's coming to her hometown to be married. Would that one act have changed anything? Would it really have made a difference in Isaac's life and in the destiny of the children of Israel? Let's look at God's instruction to Abraham in order to get a better understanding of this matter.

> *Now the LORD had said to Abram: "Get out of your country, from your family and from your father's house, to a land that I will show you. I will make you a great nation; I will bless you and make your name great; and you shall be a blessing. I will bless those who bless you, and I will curse him who curses you;*

and in you all the families of the earth shall be blessed." So Abram departed as the Lord had spoken to him, and Lot went with him. And Abram was seventy-five years old when he departed from Haran. Then Abram took Sarai his wife and Lot his brother's son, and all their possessions that they had gathered, and the people whom they had acquired in Haran, and they departed to go to the land of Canaan. So they came to the land of Canaan. Abram passed through the land to the place of Shechem, as far as the terebinth tree of Moreh. And the Canaanites were then in the land. Then the Lord appeared to Abram and said, "To your descendants I will give this land." And there he built an altar to the Lord, who had appeared to him (Genesis 12:1–7).

God specifically told Abraham to get out of his native country. He told him to get away from his family and away from his father's house. Then God promised to show Abraham a land that He would give him. That land was the land of Canaan. God promised that Abraham would become a great nation and that through his seed all the nations would be blessed.

God further told Abraham that anyone who cursed him would be cursed and all who blessed him would be blessed. Although Abraham was old and sudden relocation was not common among citizens his age, he chose to obey the voice of the Lord and went. When Abraham passed through the land of Canaan, God reminded him that this land was the land that He had reserved for his descendants. Abraham built an altar of worship unto the Lord at that very place.

Notice that Abraham had to obey. Many of God's blessings are contingent upon your obedience. Look at this Scripture for an example: *"If you are willing and obedient, you shall eat the good of the land; but if you refuse and rebel, you shall be devoured by the sword; for the mouth of the Lord has spoken"* (Isaiah 1:19–20). Willingness without obedience will not produce the desired end result. You may be obedient yet have an inner unwillingness to possess the land. In that case your obedience still does not reward you with the fruit of the land. Obedience and willingness are the two components that produce the promise. Some words that God gives us are contingent upon our doing something first to set them in motion.

God gave Abraham a promise—a lofty promise. However, that promise hinged upon Abraham's doing the one thing God told him to do: Go. If Abraham had stayed in the land of his father and family, this promise would never have come to pass. It would have never been realized. By this one act, the promise was activated.

On the other hand, if he or his family decided to go back to the land that God told them to leave, then that act alone may have nullified the promise of God. So it was highly important that Isaac's wife be a woman who had a spirit to follow, not to rebel. It may appear to be a tiny detail, but we can see just how much damage could have potentially occurred if Abraham's servant brought Isaac back to the land from which they came from. It may have disqualified the entire family from receiving the blessing of God.

One of the characteristics of God as well as of strong marriages is always looking forward and not backward. God is always reaching for new possibilities in you. He is not pondering over whatever happened in your past. Isaac's wife-to-be was fortunate in that she was going to marry a child of intention. She, by uniting with Isaac, was going to join a lineage that would become a spiritual legacy. She was marrying a true leader. Little did she know that she would bear unto her husband a son who would be the namesake of all Hebrew people.

The odds for finding a true leader for a husband appear to be against many women in our modern society. A single man who faithfully attends church, seeks God regularly in prayer, fasts for inner cleansing, and gives his time, talent, and treasure to the things of God is a rarity. Now, such a man *does* exist. However, godly men do not exist in such high numbers as to balance the scales against the men who are just the opposite or, worse, in jail.

Because many of our men are in prison, on drugs, or actively committing crimes that will sooner or later get them incarcerated, the visibility of godly men seems to be a bit obscured universally. Such neglect to spiritual values on the part of husbands and fathers has caused many women to take on the role of spiritual leaders, spearheading any and all attempts to connect to the things that are sacred. This is perhaps why women, in most circles barring few, significantly outnumber men within the local church. And this is why, within the local church, women now fill positions in all capacities, even those they were not designed to fill.

Women are looking for a man to follow. That is not a chauvinistic remark; it is a God-given response placed within the woman to follow a leader. Now, this does not diminish women in leadership; nor does it intend to imply that a woman cannot lead both in a spiritual sense and vocationally. What I am saying is that most women long for a man whom they can follow without having to worry whether or not he will lead them down a deadly path.

Abraham answered his servant, *"And if the woman is not willing to follow you, then you will be released from this oath; only do not take my son back there"* (Genesis 24:8). He freed his servant of the oath that he swore to Abraham if the woman would not follow him. Abraham's statement here signifies a powerful reality. If this woman could not follow, then she was not the right woman for Isaac. He needed to have a woman who would follow trustfully.

Abraham was submitted to the will of God and was sensitive to God's voice. He recognized that God might speak direction into his life at any time. That direction could require him to relocate or to make a sudden change in his living situation. Whatever the case, he knew that he would obey God at whatever cost. Having a wife who was not in agreement with God and His plan for his family's life would have only delayed God's overall plan and purpose for Isaac's life.

> **Most women long for a man whom they can follow without having to worry whether or not he will lead them down a deadly path.**

Knowing up front whether his wife would be a follower or one who rebelled was crucial. In the same way, because of the spontaneous character of God, His followers must always be ready to obey and act when needed. Anybody or anything that prohibits your freedom to obey God's voice should be viewed as an enemy of God. So, brother, as with Isaac, it is important to choose a woman who is willing to follow you.

But before you go off telling your girlfriend she needs to follow your lead, let me say this: It is far more important that you equip yourself with all the necessary elements and qualities that would make a woman *want* to follow you when asked. Be a leader with such intentional leadership skills and such a passion for things that are divine that when a woman follows you, it is second nature and sheer pleasure for her rather than drudgery.

THE TEST—HOSPITABLE SERVICE

And the servant ran to meet her and said, "Please let me drink a little water from your pitcher." So she said, "Drink, my lord." Then she quickly let her pitcher down to her hand, and gave him a drink. And when she had finished giving him a drink, she said, "I will draw water for your camels also, until they have finished drinking." Then she quickly emptied her pitcher into the trough, ran back to the well to draw water, and drew for all his camels. And the man, wondering at her, remained silent so as to know whether the Lord had made his journey prosperous [beneficial or worthwhile] *or not* (Genesis 24:17–21).

When Abraham's servant met Rebekah, he asked for a little water from her pitcher. Naturally he was thirsty after having traveled a long journey. But his thirst was not his sole motivation for asking her for some water. Abraham's servant was trying to determine by the girl's actions and response what type of character she possessed. Was she hospitable? Did she have the heart of a servant? Was she self-centered and unkind? Did she have a giving nature?

Questions such as these surely must have run through the servant's mind. Remember, he was entrusted with the high responsibility of selecting Isaac's wife. She had to have certain qualities. He did not have years to assess this woman and then make his decision. He had to decide within a very short amount of time. So the things that he looked for in Rebekah went far beyond the facial beauty that she possessed. He wanted to go deeper into her interior makeup to establish whether or not she would serve as a suitable mate for his lord's son.

Interestingly, the name *Rebekah* in its Arabic meaning literally means a tie rope for animals. It suggests that her beauty was so pronounced that she would snare or bind any man who looked upon her. Had the servant paid strict attention to her beauty alone and not looked for her other attributes (he too being a man), he would have been ensnared and overcome by her beauty. That, of course, would have caused him to lose his proper focus— determining her character. He had to focus on things other than her captivating beauty.

He had to hone in on her service—how she treated strangers. Why was this important? Should it have really made a difference whether she was hospitable or not? After all, she was going to be joined to a family who could afford hired servants. Why would she need to have a servant's heart? One reason could be that her attitude needed to be like the character of the Messiah who was prophesied to come. If she was going to conceive a son who would carry on a Messianic legacy, then she would have to possess the same characteristics of what she expected to be born from her womb.

Some say it like this: Like begets like. Everything produces after its own kind. Wicked produces wicked and righteous produces righteous. Throughout the entire New Testament there are many references to Jesus' being a servant of the people. His servanthood is perhaps one of His most noted character traits that are celebrated to this very day. *"The God of Abraham, Isaac, and Jacob, the God of our fathers, glorified His Servant Jesus, whom you delivered up and denied in the presence of Pilate, when he was determined to let Him go"* (Acts 3:13). Furthermore, Rebekah's character of service would set the pace for several key events that were to happen throughout the course of her marriage and beyond.

To the servant's delight, not only did she give him water, but she also offered to draw water for his camels. She was willing to go above and beyond what she was asked to do. Not only did she give the man drink, but his camels as well. She wanted to make sure that they drank until they were no longer thirsty. She gladly continued to draw water until they were satisfied.

By just this simple act Abraham's servant realized that this virgin woman had some valuable character traits. She had a heart to serve. There is a difference between having a heart to serve and serving out of force. He discovered that it was Rebekah's nature to serve. It wasn't against her will. When you serve because you want to serve, you will gladly continue serving. However, when you have been coerced into serving, you will last only until your service is over.

> So it was, when the camels had finished drinking, that the man took a golden nose ring weighing half a shekel, and two bracelets for her wrists weighing ten shekels of gold, and said, "Whose daughter are you? Tell me, please, is there room in your father's house for us to lodge?" So she said to him, "I am the daughter of Bethuel, Milcah's son, whom she bore to Nahor." Moreover she said to him, "We have both straw and feed enough, and room to lodge." Then the man bowed down his head and worshiped the Lord (Genesis 24:22–26).

Realizing that she was the prime choice for Isaac, he asked her whose daughter she was. During that era it was customary for the groom's family to ask the girl's father permission for his daughter to be married. Without her father's consent she would not have been released to him. In addition, the servant had to bring a dowry on behalf of the groom to compensate the father for having to replace part of his domestic workforce.

After she told the servant who her father was, she informed him that there was room for him to stay with them and that they had an adequate supply of food for his animals. In short, she offered hospitality. There were no more questions needed. Immediately

Abraham's servant bowed down in reverence to God and began to worship the Lord. Had he chosen the wrong woman it would have cost his life. So he expressed gratitude and thanks to God for leading him to the right one.

Remember, child of promise, not just any mate will do. Don't look at the outward appearance, but at the inner qualities. Modify your requirements for your future spouse, if need be. Is that man a leader? Is that woman willing to follow? Is he or she willing to serve? Are *you* hospitable? It's not the outside, but the inside that counts.

Chapter Four

The Proverbs 31 Woman

For centuries scholars and Bible lovers have esteemed chapter 31 of Proverbs as the standard by which all women should measure themselves. Verses 10 through 31 specifically identify the characteristics of a woman of virtue. Through this biblical example we will gather a much broader and comprehensive definition of what exactly it means to be a virtuous woman.

This beautiful passage clearly pinpoints various traits that this godly woman possessed—characteristics that we often overlook today. So often people focus on *virtue* as relating to chastity, but this woman's virtue went far beyond sexual morality. So, brother, if you are looking for a godly woman, then here is your standard. Sister, here is your goal of what you can become. This is God's best for you and in you.

THE SEARCH CONTINUES

Who can find a virtuous wife? (Proverbs 31:10)

This question alone is loaded for bear. It holds more meaning than most people actually realize. As I mentioned before, we expect a virtuous woman to be sexually faithful to her spouse and in good moral standing with God, but the meaning of *virtuous* goes beyond merely being sexually pure.

In no way do I minimize the great value of a woman maintaining her virginity. On the contrary, I applaud her and encourage all women (and men!) to do the same. I simply want to emphasize that sexual propriety is just *one* of many things that a woman of virtue possesses in order for her to receive the high honor of such a name. Maintaining virginity alone does not automatically quali-fy a woman as a Proverbs 31 woman of virtue.

The meaning of *virtuous* goes beyond merely being sexually pure.

In fact, there are many women who, though they lost their virginity at an early age due to ignorance and lack of biblical teaching, later attained the status of being virtuous women by following the princi-ples in God's Word. Yes, there is still hope for the woman who has failed. The grace and mercy of God allow men and women to turn around and start afresh as if their negative past never hap-pened at all.

In order to get a better understanding of all the qualities that a virtuous woman exhibits, let us look at a proper definition of the word *virtuous*.

The word for "virtuous" in the Hebrew is *chayil*. It conveys the meaning of force, as in the force of an army.[1] The connotation is that this woman has behind her a force of strength, courage, and a natural propensity to create wealth with limited resources. She possesses great ingenuity. It does not say anything about morality.

There is nothing at all that suggests moral excellence alone within its original meaning. Yet, when most people think of a vir-tuous woman, that's usually the first and only attribute that is looked for. Now, heaven knows how much moral excellence is des-perately needed in our morally declining culture. The problem with the more modern definition of virtuous is that it nearly nulli-fies the original meaning of the word. *Virtuous* and *virgin* are two different concepts. Being a virgin deals more with the outward and physical interaction with another person.

Being a virtuous woman, however, goes even deeper. It seeks to identify inward qualities and character traits that, like fine wine, become more valuable with time. Of the many characteristics of a virtuous woman, we will look at these: strength and courage,

---

1.   James Strong, *Strong's Exhaustive Concordance of the Bible* (Nashville, Ten-nessee: Holman Bible Publishers, n.d.), #H2428.

entrepreneurship, value, trustworthiness, industriousness, generosity, given to teaching, and wisdom.

Strength and Courage

The virtuous woman possesses incessant strength. She is an example to those around her not only of how to be strong against all odds, but also of how to remain strong. If there is one thing that every man needs, it is a strong woman. A strong woman knows who she is. She knows that God, her Creator, has defined who she is. Thus other people's opinions and estimations of her mean nothing to her.

This woman does not need to compete with other women; nor does she clamor for attention. She knows her true worth. It would be embarrassing for her to crave appreciation, since she knows that God created her with a uniqueness that only He could imprint within her spirit.

When tragedy and hard times come, this strong woman bounces back into the game of life without fail. Her strength and endurance send a much-needed message to her enemies that she is built to last.

Her opposite is a woman who has become very familiar to many men. The woman lacking virtue suffers from incredibly low self-esteem. She constantly needs the approval of everyone, especially men. This woman is an emotional wreck; the simplest, most trivial issues seem to bother her and can easily run her off course. When bad times come, everyone knows it because her appearance shows it. She displays in every way that her life depends on a man rather than on the Lord. Society at large has rightly labeled this woman as a needy person.

A virtuous woman, however, has courage in addition to strength. She is a woman of dauntless courage, and she displays it with honor. The Scriptures tell the stories of many such women— women who possessed great courage in the face of adversity. Queen Esther was one. Her courageous act literally set the destiny for the entire Jewish nation of her day. At the risk of her own life,

Esther went into the king's court uninvited and eventually obtained a reversal of the decree issued against the Jews.

She could have lost her life in pursuit of this goal, yet she persisted. *"For whoever desires to save his life will lose it, but whoever loses his life for My sake will find it"* (Matthew 16:25). Determined to save her nation's posterity, she made the decision that even if she died in the process, the fight for life was worth it all.

> *Go, gather all the Jews who are present in Shushan, and fast for me; neither eat nor drink for three days, night or day. My maids and I will fast likewise.* ***And so I will go to the king, which is against the law; and if I perish, I perish!*** (Esther 4:16, emphasis added)

Educator, playwright, poet, and best-selling author of *I Know Why the Caged Bird Sings*, Maya Angelou has said that a person isn't born with courage, but with the *potential* to pursue courage. She also said that courage is necessary to successfully live out any other virtue. That is so true. A Proverbs 31 woman may not be born with courage, yet she recognizes the need for courage and pursues it, knowing that she will never build anything of worth or lasting value without it.

A CREATIVE ENTREPRENEUR

> *She seeks wool and flax, and willingly works with her hands. She is like the merchant ships, she brings her food from afar....She considers a field and buys it; from her profits she plants a vineyard....She stretches out her hands to the distaff, and her hand holds the spindle....She makes linen garments and sells them, and supplies sashes for the merchants* (Proverbs 31:13–14,16,19,24).

A virtuous woman has an innate ability to create wealth. She is not a lazy woman but one who recognizes opportunities and does not hesitate to capitalize on each one. During the Great Depression in the United States of America, which began in 1929 and lasted through most of the 1930s, many women used their resourcefulness to help bring income into their households.

Women would cook pies, bake cakes, clean homes, make clothes out of raw materials, and sell vegetables all in exchange for money or bartered goods. A good cook could take a few potatoes and chicken neck bones and create a soup that not only tasted great but also was enough to feed a growing family of often more than ten persons. How could such a virtuous woman still have money and food when everyone else complained of the worst economic conditions in history at the time? The answer is simple: She was empowered by God to create wealth.

And you shall remember the Lord your God, for it is He who gives you power to get wealth, that He may establish His covenant which He swore to your fathers, as it is this day (Deuteronomy 8:18).

The virtuous woman is industrious. She knows how to manage little and believe God to increase what little she has until it becomes much. This woman knows well the power of the law of use that says, "Use it or lose it." She understands basic concepts of operating a business. Knowing that she has the responsibility to provide nutritious meals for her family and be a helper to her husband, she is compelled to find creative and imaginative ways to increase in every area of her life. She knows that if she passes God's test with little, He is obliged to give her more.

His lord said to him, "Well done, good and faithful servant; you have been faithful over a few things, I will make you ruler over many things. Enter into the joy of your lord" (Matthew 25:23).

I believe that the greatest virtue this woman in Proverbs 31 had was her understanding that none of these things could ever happen for her without God's favor. So a virtuous woman lives in constant pursuit of God, knowing that without Him failure is inevitable. How else could a woman create wealth during an economically depressed time? It just doesn't make sense otherwise.

How can a woman walk in strength and courage when she is faced with a major problem that many would slowly crumble under? Just how can a woman continue to be creative in every area of life sexually, spiritually, and physically when the world around her throws major distractions her way? In the natural realm, none of these things is possible.

A virtuous woman lives in constant pursuit of God.

A woman having such enormous challenges could easily become a candidate for emotional and mental breakdown. Not the Proverbs 31 woman. She finds her peace and provision in her daily pursuit of God. She loves the Lord with all her heart and soul. Her true first love is neither toward her husband nor her children. Her first love is with her Creator, God the Father. She will not let anything come in between her and God. That's what makes her different. That is what makes her virtuous.

> *As the deer pants for streams of water, so my soul pants for you, O God. My soul thirsts for God, for the living God. When can I go and meet with God? My tears have been my food day and night, while men say to me all day long, "Where is your God?" These things I remember as I pour out my soul: how I used to go with the multitude, leading the procession to the house of God, with shouts of joy and thanksgiving among the festive throng* (Psalm 42:1–4 NIV).

MORE PRECIOUS THAN DIAMONDS

> *Who can find a virtuous wife? For her worth is far above rubies* (Proverbs 31:10).

What is a diamond, today's coveted gemstone, worth? What would the choicest, rarest, finest quality diamond in the world cost? Perhaps such a stone would be valued in the millions. Yet, when you compare the finest diamond to a virtuous wife, her value makes the diamond seem nearly worthless in comparison. The Bible says, *"For her worth is far above rubies."*

What's so interesting about this concept is that the writer of this proverb began by informing the reader that this woman is a woman of virtue—which has multiple meanings. After that is established in the mind of the reader, the writer immediately shifts the attention from what she is to what she is worth. The next important information is *her value*. The proverb compares this woman's value to one of the most valuable commodities of that day—a ruby.

A ruby then was as valuable as a choice diamond is now. It is argued that some rubies are harder (in terms of density) than diamonds, and that therefore rubies are the hardest and most precious of all stones. Either way, the point is that a virtuous lady is priceless. The man who finds a virtuous wife should consider her to be his most valuable asset, knowing that he can never earn her true worth. She is truly inestimable.

That is why a real lady should never cheapen herself by displaying lewd and licentious behavior. She should always practice behavior that is in direct proportion to her cost. Have you ever wondered why the number of children born to unwed parents is rising ever so speedily? The reason is not necessarily what you think. It is not because girls have an unrestrained desire to engage in sexual intercourse with whosoever will.

More often it is because women who have not been properly fathered or carefully mentored are in search of purpose and self. The woman who does not know who she is because her father neglected to speak purpose into her life will always search for a man who will. Unfortunately, most of the time the person who volunteers to take on the "father" role is not a godly man.

Such men are usually ones assigned by the devil to ruin the life of many women. You see it all the time. You see young women with low self-esteem who do not know their true value, dressed skimpily and hanging on the street corners or at the shopping mall in search of any man who will show them some attention. These same needy women often join the nightclub scene every weekend looking to meet someone who will fill the void.

It does not matter one whit whether she is absolutely beautiful or not. She could even be tremendously smart, possessing keen intellectual insight. Looks don't matter. Intelligence doesn't matter either. On the inside, where it counts the most, she is as wide and empty as the space between the walls of the Grand Canyon, making it ever so easy for anyone to enter into her life. What she really needs cannot come from a man. It cannot come from having great and enjoyable sex. No matter how much "extracurricular" time she spends with her so-called lover, she will still want more. What she needs most can come only from the One who fashioned her with His own hands—God.

Just as a diamond must be in the hands of a skilled diamond appraiser in order for the value of that stone to be known, so a lady of virtue must be placed in the company of godly people for them to properly estimate her worth. What is a diamond worth in the presence of pigs? It is worth very little to the pig, I'm sure. What would a pig do with a diamond? It would only trample the diamond beneath its feet, grinding the gem into the mud and manure.

Does the pig intentionally devalue the diamond, or has the pig simply not been trained to know the value of it? I don't believe it's intentional. You just cannot expect a pig to know any better. Woman of virtue, please realize that there are few skilled appraisers trained by the Master to value you at fair market value. Avoid the trap of subjecting yourself to the opinions or appraisal of any man. Only God knows your ultimate worth.

If you doubt your true value, don't ask another man for his opinion. He may be able to see you only with limited vision. See yourself as God sees you…as priceless. Don't lower your standard. You are a woman of virtue, a woman of excellence, a woman of impeccable taste, a woman without cost, and a woman of God. Never forget it!

SHE CAN BE TRUSTED

The heart of her husband safely trusts her; so he will have no lack of gain. She does him good and not evil all the days of her life (Proverbs 31:11–12).

We live in a time in which *trust* has become an antiquated word of past ages. Although many people continually abuse the trust others put in them, it is still a virtue that should be expected from everyone, particularly from those with integrity. Unfortunately, scandals from the pulpits of the Catholic Church to the boardrooms of the Enron Corporation clearly show that trust has become an unimportant issue in the minds of those holding offices of high esteem.

Nevertheless, God still expects you to honor the trust put in you. He expects you to still trust others. It is a virtue that the Proverbs 31 woman lived by, for she was trusted not by mere strangers but by the one to whom she gave her hand in marriage. A trustworthy wife is very important. Likewise, a wife who trusts her husband is an incomparable blessing. When I was a young traveling minister, older preachers informed me that my preaching was only as powerful as my wife's amen. If my wife could not say amen, then all the other accolades really did not matter. This constructive criticism has greatly helped me and my marriage.

You see, I sleep with her. I regularly eat with her. My most intimate moments in life are shared with the wife of my youth. It seems only reasonable to consider her feelings, emotions, and opinions before anyone else's. Her trusting me and my trusting her are at the top of our relational priorities. The husband of the woman in Proverbs 31 carefully entrusted her with his very own heart—his innermost being. Such trust should never be freely given to just any soul.

When you study this passage in Proverbs, you'll notice that this woman was trusted not with frivolous matters but with major areas of her husband's fortune. He had great confidence that he could leave his house for an extended period of time and it would only prosper in his absence. His children would remain honorable citizens in the eyes of the community. His financial obligations would be paid on time. His house would be kept clean, the landscaping well tended, and his hired help paid.

His household would not miss a beat. No one would ever know that he was not at home because his wife managed his affairs with the spirit of excellence. This issue of trust is a great one. So many women ruin a man's home and financial stability in just moments.

I am reminded of a church-going woman in the New England area who is married to an unsaved man. They have been married for approximately forty-five years. Her husband is an extremely hardworking, blue-collar factory worker. For years each week he would give his wife his entire paycheck, trusting that she would pay all the bills on time. He suffered with alcoholism pretty badly, so he didn't trust himself to hold onto all the money that he earned each week. His church-going wife would give him between forty to fifty dollars each week. That money went mostly for his lunch purchases. Whatever was left over went toward his drinking habit.

About sixty percent of the time, she would pay all the bills in a timely manner. However, whenever there was a state or national church convention near her home, she would not use the money to pay for any of the bills. Instead she purchased clothes and big fancy hats with matching shoes and clutches so she could look as if she was the most prosperous woman in the convention.

As a result, their electricity was cut off all the time. They received numerous foreclosure warnings from the bank. Often they had to cut firewood to heat the cold house since their gas bill was not paid on time. They even had times when no dinner sat on the table and the husband went on swearing and cursing fits because his hunger was not satisfied. Instead of buying groceries, she bought clothes.

No matter how much her husband argued, fought, and complained to her about it, she continued to do the same thing over and over. She thought that she was justified in her actions because her husband wasn't saved. She thought these actions would be his punishment or maybe the needed pressure to convince him to accept God. To my knowledge her husband has still not accepted Jesus Christ as his Savior. Because of her prodigal example, her husband may never be born again...simply because she cannot be trusted.

A virtuous woman does not waste money, regardless if it's her money or her husband's. She possesses a frugal character and always looks for opportunities to save and conserve, preparing for days ahead. Simple things like properly balancing a checkbook, having a savings account (with money in it), cutting out coupons, and paying bills before they are due and not after are just a few practical clues to a woman's trustworthiness in household matters.

In addition, the virtuous woman's time is well accounted for. She does not have time to engage in an extramarital affair or to gossip with male-bashing, disgruntled women. She is always in hot pursuit of running the affairs of her home well. She knows that what she does or does not do could make or break everything that she and her husband have built together. She takes this trust issue very seriously because she knows that she is accountable for all her deeds to God and her husband.

TAKING CARE OF THE HOME FRONT

She also rises while it is yet night, and provides food for her household, and a portion for her maidservants (Proverbs 31:15).

There was a time when it was an understood requirement that a woman know how to cook, and cook well. That day seems to have long disappeared. We live in a time now in which women are just as skilled, far smarter, and as competitive in the marketplace as men are. As a result, women cannot perform the domestic duties that once went hand in hand with being a woman.

Although this is fact, there is nothing inherently wrong with it. I applaud a woman who has a money-making capacity in her hands. This Proverbs 31 woman was a prosperous businesswoman too. She managed a multifaceted operation, yet at the same time she did not fail to minister to the needs of her household. She somehow found the balance between the two (business and home) so that neither area lacked.

I am not saying that women must become full-time cooks in order to have happy marriages or to be pleasing to God. What I am saying is that your man still needs to eat. You should not put your marriage relationship in a position that may give the devil an opportunity to wreak havoc. It is foolish to allow another woman's cooking and domestic excellence to become more enticing than yours.

Now let me add some balance to all this. Couples vary in terms of their financial status. Some are able to eat out at fancy upscale restaurants every night. Others may have private, full-time chefs in their homes. Many others struggle to make the best of what little they have. Far more people fall into this last category, particularly newlyweds. Sometimes the husband can cook better than the wife can! (Men particularly from the Caribbean Islands have been reared as master cooks from the time they were young boys!) If that applies to you, then you will make concessions based on that—a little give and a little take. Every situation is different. My concern is that the woman care enough to ensure that her man and children always have healthy and filling meals. That obligation should never be given to "the other woman."

SHE GIVES GENEROUSLY TO ALL WHO ARE IN NEED

She extends her hand to the poor, yes, she reaches out her hands to the needy (Proverbs 31:20).

What a heart! This woman has a heart for those who are less privileged than she is. She has pity on the poor. It is obvious that she has plenty, since she shares what she has with others. It is also obvious that the principle of sowing and reaping is in action. This is one of the reasons she will never be without—she chooses to bless others.

Do not be deceived, God is not mocked; for whatever a man sows, that he will also reap (Galatians 6:7).

Now may He who supplies seed to the sower, and bread for food, supply and multiply the seed you have sown and increase the fruits of your righteousness, while you are enriched in everything for all liberality, which causes thanksgiving through us to God (2 Corinthians 9:10–11).

Although the Proverbs 31 woman has the responsibility of caring for her family, she freely takes on the responsibility of providing for others as well. She is a mother not only to her biological children, but also to the community at large. Those who are hungry know that this woman has enough compassion in her heart to feed them and not selfishly send them away wanting.

It is interesting to note that this virtuous woman never runs short of any raw materials or ingredients to accomplish what she sets out to do. She always seems to have enough, much like the widow woman in 1 Kings 17, whose cruse of oil never dried up during the famine or the meal ever got low.

The widow in Zarephath, in a similar way, cared about the needs of the prophet Elijah. Because she put his sustenance before hers, God opened an avenue for a continual supernatural supply in her and her son's life. Such a massive provision might never have been possible if she had not chosen to reach out to others. Thank God these virtuous women made the right choice.

So she went away and did according to the word of Elijah; and she and he and her household ate for many days. The bin of flour was not used up, nor did the jar of oil run dry, according to the word of the Lord which He spoke by Elijah (1 Kings 17:15–16).

She Teaches Her Children Well

Her children rise up and call her blessed; her husband also, and he praises her: "Many daughters have done well, but you excel them all" (Proverbs 31:28–29).

What your children think of you has great weight. It even may have more weight than you actually realize. After all, these children have been in your company every day of your life for nearly two decades. They know the real you and can make a proper assessment of who you really are and what you truly stand for. Children have an instinctive ability to distinguish hypocrites from those who are genuine.

Over the years children get the opportunity to prove if your words really mean anything. They know what you truly believe because they get to see it practiced or not practiced before them every single day. You cannot tell children one thing, yet do another. They will be utterly dissatisfied. What you say out of your mouth you must practice in your lifestyle. If you do not, you will never recruit them into your army. You should live what you preach before them.

The implication in this Scripture is that her children are not little babies or toddlers. If they were small children, it would make no sense to include them in this passage. Think about it. Most young children instinctively praise their mothers; it is a natural thing for them to do. Babies cry for their mothers whether their mothers are good-natured or cross.

Simply because her baby cries for her shouldn't make the mother all puffed up. She shouldn't become proud in the belief that she is doing an above-average job in mothering her child. Even if a mother doesn't properly feed her child, that child may cry for its mother. It's not because the mother is doing a great job. It is just what small children do.

But when your grown children, who have witnessed your triumphs and defeats, can still call you blessed—that is highly commendable. This woman's children must have seen examples of other mothers who they would not call blessed. They had to have had something to use as a comparison. After they saw other examples— perhaps some better and some worse—they were still able to say of their mother, "You are blessed." You are blessed, Mother— empowered to prosper no matter the season in life.

Whether in famine or harvest, in time of war or peace, whether under great pressure or in the midst of the fire, this mother still progressed forward. That speaks volumes about her character, her tenacity, and her moral strength. She trained her children well. This mother who knew the fear of the Lord raised her children to have a reverence and holy fear for God as well.

The virtuous woman knows all too well that if she instills values of righteousness in her children from a young age, she will never have to worry about their prosperity. She will never have to worry about their straying or whoring after false gods. Unlike many mothers in our busy culture, the Proverbs 31 woman took quality time to teach her children values that could only come from the heart of a godly mother. For this reason, they called her blessed.

> *Train up a child in the way he should go, and when he is old he will not depart from it* (Proverbs 22:6).

A WOMAN OF UNQUESTIONABLE WISDOM

> *This is my conclusion, says the Preacher. Step by step I came to this result after researching in every direction: One tenth of one percent of the men I interviewed could be said to be wise, but not one woman!* (Ecclesiastes 7:27–28 TLB).

> *Charm is deceitful and beauty is passing, but a woman who fears the Lord, she shall be praised* (Proverbs 31:30).

There is a major difference between being smart and being wise. Sad to say, many people regularly confuse the two, usually to their detriment. Smartness deals with mental intelligence, with understanding facts and figures, concepts and illustrations. Yet, wisdom is far greater than smartness because it gives a person the know-how to apply what was learned.

I have heard unwise yet academically smart women humiliate their husbands. These women have said to their husbands in public places, "You're stupid. That doesn't make any sense. I hold a degree in law. I'm a medical doctor, buddy. I graduated with honors; you barely made it out of high school." And so on. The list of insults I have heard would fill the pages of several volumes of books.

Sadly, for these women, most real men will not stay around too long. They won't long endure such degrading talk. Now, it is a wonderful thing to be an educated woman. I believe every woman should pursue an education if for no other reason than just to stretch the human mind. However, some women (not all) spend years in school earning degrees to compensate for their poor self-images.

These women undoubtedly educate themselves for the wrong reasons—they use those initials after their names as some sort of ammunition against men who lack formal education. This is unwise, dear sisters. Every educated woman should use her God-given influence, sexuality, and wisdom to encourage her husband to increase in knowledge. It should be her aim to make sure that her husband comes up several levels in life mainly because she's in his life.

Marriage is all about enhancing each other. It is about strengthening your partner in the area in which he or she may be weak. Using wisdom means that you continually seek God as to how you should speak to one another, how to introduce new concepts and ideas to each other, and when to speak from when to close your mouth. This latter skill is extremely important. Millions of homes have been destroyed because unwise women were more skilled at tearing things down than building them up. Remember, any fool can tear a building down. But only a wise person knows how to construct a building.

The wise woman builds her house, but the foolish pulls it down with her hands (Proverbs 14:1).

A marriage can last for a lifetime when both parties choose to use wisdom. A little wisdom goes a long way. Use wisdom in how you speak to one another. The tone and volume of your voice, the expressions on your face, and the attitude in which you confront your partner all matters. *"A soft answer turns away wrath, but a harsh word stirs up anger"* (Proverbs 15:1).

There are times when Beverly wants to tell me something that has been bothering her. It may be right after preaching a sermon, when I need to be spiritually and physically replenished. It may be at a time when I am dealing with a serious issue at the ministry. Perhaps my boys are just being boys at a time when I need peaceful

Marriage is all about enhancing each other.

thought. My wife uses the wisdom within her to know when is the proper time to share her concern with me.

I am not saying that my wife doesn't have open access to me at all times; she does. But using wisdom in cases like that just helps the overall flow of the situation. If there were a possibility for confusion and senseless misunderstandings to take place, then by using wisdom she averts those things. I believe that God expects us to use wisdom in every area of our lives, especially in the area of marriage.

It's no mistake that Solomon spoke so much of wisdom in the Book of Proverbs. King Solomon was a master lover. He was a woman's man. He understood relationships in a way that few today understand. The Song of Solomon expresses how well he could serenade a woman by making mention of things that many men neglect or overlook. This king knew what to say and how to say it. Yet, when he penned his many proverbs, the consistent theme was about wisdom. In fact, he stated that wisdom should be everyone's chief concern.

> *Wisdom is the principal thing; therefore get wisdom. And in all your getting, get understanding. Exalt her, and she will promote you; she will bring you honor, when you embrace her* (Proverbs 4:7–8).

Not just any wisdom will do, however. Truly much great wisdom has emerged from the minds of humankind. Although this kind of wisdom has built great nations, large cities, and sprawling empires, in some cases it has destroyed them as well. Wisdom that comes from God, on the other hand, has a phenomenal track record of producing that which lasts.

It is this God-kind of wisdom that causes churches to endure, families to persist through the toughest of times, and marriages to last forever. But, this kind of wisdom can be acquired only after you begin to fear the Lord. At this point (the point of having a reverential fear of God) your wisdom has only just begun.

> *The fear of the Lord is the beginning of wisdom; a good understanding have all those who do His commandments. His praise endures forever* (Psalm 111:10).

Dear sister, married or unmarried, you can start right now to become a woman of virtue. When you pursue God and follow His kingdom, you'll become far more priceless in a man's eyes than any other valuable he possesses. And, brother, to deserve your woman of virtue, you need to study to become a mighty man of valor.

Chapter Five

A Mighty Man of Valor

One of the increasingly noticeable trends in our society is lop-sided relationships. Far too many women appear to have it all to-gether, yet in a moment of desperation connect with a weak man. Why?

Virtuous women should desire mighty men of valor, and vice versa. No woman should desire to spend her life with a weak man. How does she recognize such a man when she meets him? How does a man become mighty in valor? This chapter will help you, sister, to recognize such a man. Brother, if you want to im-prove yourself, keep reading. Within your reach are valuable skills and principles that will catapult you to a totally new dimension of living.

I WANT A NEW ME

Do you want a new you? In order for that to happen, two things must take place. First, the man must become totally dissat-isfied with his weakness. Now, I'm not suggesting that if you have given an area of weakness over to the Lord that you allow that to hinder your progress. If your weakness is under the blood, that is exactly where we will leave it.

No, the thing that men must become dissatisfied with is their *allowing* themselves to become weak. Ask yourself, "Why am I not a mighty man of valor? What could I do right now that will begin pointing me in the right direction toward becoming that mighty man of valor?" Change never happens until you recognize there is a need. This is a challenge for men—many don't realize that they need to change.

Convincing men that their lives could be better, that they could have more in life, and that they can get far more out of life can at times be a worthless pursuit. Too many men have become comfortable with being the losers that they are. Unfortunately, because of the lack of fathers in our generation, many men simply have not had a model of manhood before them.

Added to that is the problem of incarceration, especially within the African-American male community. *Hope* for many black men in the prison systems has become a fantasy that seems to be as unreachable as a passing star. And that only exacerbates the situation.

Nevertheless, for men both in and out of prison, the first step is to admit that they need help and become teachable enough to seek and receive that help.

The second thing that needs to take place is women to stop pampering their men.

> *For even when we were with you, we commanded you this: If anyone will not work, neither shall he eat* (2 Thessalonians 3:10).

> *The lazy man does not roast what he took in hunting, but diligence is man's precious possession* (Proverbs 12:27).

Women in general must stop babying the men by becoming their enablers. The word *enabler* has become a common phrase in popular society and is associated mostly with drug addiction. It refers to people who enable or help to support or compensate dysfunctional human behavior such as drug addiction and alcoholism. Although those types of addictions are obviously destructive, there are other behavior patterns that are equally as crippling.

For example, laziness will destroy manhood. There are some women who enable this behavior by financially supporting a man. I am not referring to men who are mentally handicapped or physically challenged in some way. Those disabilities can excuse a husband from this scenario, though not always. There are men who are physically or mentally challenged yet work jobs every single day.

I am talking about well able, strong-bodied men who refuse to work a job because they don't have to. All their needs are being taken care of by a woman. Their jeans, sneakers, sweatshirts, socks, and underwear are all purchased by their female enablers. Their food is purchased and prepared for them by these enablers three times a day.

If these men need money for travel or entertainment, such as going to the movies or eating out, they know that they can easily get an interest-free, non-payable, long-term loan from their enablers. "What is the problem?" these men ask. "We are not asking them to do all this for us, so what difference should it make?" The problem is that until this careless behavior pattern is confronted and corrected, it will continue to cycle around.

When it becomes acceptable for a man to stay at home and for a woman to take care of him, then the mind-set of society at large slowly begins to shift to accommodate this type of insanity. We will begin to believe that it's normal. Worse yet, women will begin to believe that it is absolutely okay to financially support a man who chooses not to do anything of worth because he simply does not have to.

Sister, don't get angry at me for saying women are the chief enablers of lazy, unprofitable men. In most cases women are not the *root cause* for this situation, but they are an *ongoing cause* for the lack of strong men. Don't kill me yet—let me clarify what I mean before you draw your weapons.

Many reasons exist for why the men within our society are the way they are. I believe the primary cause is the lack of real fathers in our generation. That is where it starts, and restoring fatherhood is the only way we can totally eradicate laziness from society. Fatherlessness constitutes the vast or greater portion of the reason for the lack of men of valor. There are lesser yet just as significant problems that help to contribute as well.

Some of these are environmental and regional; some are educational and economic in their scope. What I am trying to convey, however, is that the enabling, the support system that women

Restoring fatherhood is the only way we can totally eradicate laziness from society.

provide, is the main reason such behavior *continues* and is not only tolerated but widely *accepted as normal*. You can start a fire many different ways. However, enough high-pressure water will put most fires out. If you do not apply the water, then the fire will only grow stronger and destroy everything in its path.

If women do not apply the pressure of tough love and of demanding men to be real men, then the fire of fatherlessness, child neglect, illegitimacy, and spousal abandonment will continue to destroy lives in untold amounts. The enabling must come to a shrieking halt in order for mighty men of valor to be processed and developed.

If you don't fan the fiery flame, in time it will die. In like manner, if women will begin to close their doors to enabling men, in time lazy men will die out. But don't worry—when they die, like Jesus they will come alive with a greater glory than ever. So the next time that man comes asking for a handout, give him the same answer the drug rallies of the 1980s touted: just say no!

JEROBOAM—A MIGHTY MAN OF INDUSTRY

The man Jeroboam was a mighty man of valor; and Solomon, seeing that the young man was industrious, made him the officer over all the labor force of the house of Joseph (1 Kings 11:28).

Much can be said about Jeroboam, who became the first king of Israel (as a separate nation from Judah). The Scriptures record many details about his very full life. But long before he became king, long before the revolt occurred that caused him to become king, long before Ahijah prophesied the dynasty that he would lead, long before all of that, King Solomon noticed him.

It was not his good looks or his physical attributes that got him such unsolicited attention. Not even his wisdom and intellectual prowess were the reason. Rather, Solomon noticed Jeroboam because he was an industrious man. Jeroboam was skilled in knowing not only how to perform laborious tasks with excellence, but also how to lead other people to do the same.

Here was a young man who knew how to lead other people. By his example and his own model he showed others how to build the city. This man was promoted because he had an industrious spirit. More than that, Jeroboam was called a mighty man of valor. It takes courage to lead others. A lot of people don't have that courage. I've heard people who go into business for themselves say things like, "I don't want to lead others because it's just to difficult. You just can't seem to get people to cooperate. Trying to help others eventually causes you to lose, and I don't want that to happen. I'll just work alone."

In other words, these people do not want to be "bothered" by trying to get others to see the vision and join in. They'd rather just work by themselves. It is true that it is far more difficult to convince others that they should do what you do, than to just do it yourself. However, mighty men of valor do not look at the odds. They don't look at the downside. Mighty men of valor courageously look in the face of challenge and welcome it.

This same need for courage applies to pastors and spiritual leaders. Some pastors shy away from growth particularly when they operate their churches like mom-and-pop businesses. They are intimidated by the challenge of change and the new dynamics that growth inevitably brings about. They choose and in some cases intentionally do things that will keep the church small. They just do not possess the courage it takes to manage the masses of people who are from varying backgrounds and cultural experiences. They'd rather not grow.

Mighty men of valor courageously look in the face of challenge and welcome it.

This same industrious quality is desperately needed in the family unit. Every woman needs a man who has a desire to build his family and create a financial empire for his family to live on. A man becomes far more valuable in a woman's eyes when he uses his wisdom or strength to create answers to long-standing problems. For most women this is a major turn-on. And it should be.

God has deposited inside every man the seed of wisdom for winning in life. Every man has the ability to create wealth. Of course, all the men in society will not reach this zenith of fiscal delight, but practically all men have the spiritual access to become whatever their hearts desire. As I mentioned earlier, the best thing that could ever happen to a man is for his freebie source to be cut off.

As long as a man has a continual flow of financial and daily provisions given to him, he will never work for them. Worse yet, he will never think for himself—and thinking is crucial to growth, development, discovery, industry, and wealth. So if a man does not have the opportunity to think, then he will never find the solutions that rest inside him. But, once his handout supply is cut off and all his enabling system shut down, he will be forced to find a way. He'll have to think.

That is the position most men need to be in. We need to be in a place where we must rely on the strengths, gifts, and abilities that God has freely given us. Only when we get to this point will we ever sense the need to be men of industry.

Every man has the ability to create wealth.

Let's look at an example. Suppose your mortgage payment comes due and the man of the house has mismanaged his funds, resulting in late fees and delinquency. What should a wife do? Should she instinctively feel that it is her responsibility to search for employment to dig their family out of the money trouble? Or should she encourage the husband to borrow the money from some loan source? Is she obligated at all?

A wife's primary obligation is to live her life and be such a godly example before her husband that he cannot help but come into alignment with his proper purposes and actions. In this case, bailing him out would only worsen the situation. It would never force him to search for solutions.

In fact, if the wife gets a job to take care of the husband's mess, then she is only making room for him to continue to behave irresponsibly all the time. It is kind of like giving him a license to do so. From that perspective, a woman would not be helping her husband build a household and a future together. Rather, she would be lending her hands to help him tear down everything that both worked so hard to build. Allowing the man to *think* could avert all this destruction.

Thinking precedes great industry. Every great world industry was pioneered by an industrious man or woman. Their ability and decision to use their minds created many of the useful tools, inventions, and fineries that we enjoy today. Consider Lee Iacocca, the CEO of the Chrysler company. Iacocca paid his dues climbing to the top of the Ford Motor company and becoming its president— only to lose his position eight years later in a fight for power and control that could have destroyed him.

His frustration led him to think. His thinking produced industrious solutions that eventually changed the course of the automobile industry forever. After his dispute with Mr. Ford, Iacocca went on to pioneer the design for the minivan for the Chrysler company that brought untold billions of dollars in revenue. He took a company from near bankruptcy to paying off a 1.2 billion-dollar loan and becoming one of the most profitable automobile corporations in the world.

How was Iacocca able to rebound? The answer is that he was allowed to think. His frustration drove him to creation. And we (the American consumers) paid him well for his creation. Every man has the potential to be industrious given the right opportunity and infrastructure. The reason so many men frown at the opportunity is because it takes time and dedication to be industrious. Unfortunately, most men prefer to become a part of an already existing system rather than create one because of the courageous spirit required to lead people.

It is no different in a household. It is easy and most enjoyable to conceive children. However, it takes a mighty man of valor to raise those children in the fear of the Lord. It takes courage to train those children to become lenders and not borrowers. It takes mighty courage to train children to become entrepreneurs and leaders in their respective professions. It takes courage because your wife and your children look at you first to provide the example for them to follow.

If you cannot do that, they will still follow you, but they will do so reluctantly. If you can provide that courageous example, your wife and children will live with confidence, knowing that their husband and father has given them a wealthy inheritance—an inheritance that can be passed down for many generations to come. Men—get some desires. Have ambition. Set lofty goals. Then pursue them. Do it for yourself. Do it for your God. Do it for your family. Just remember that it all starts with being industrious.

> **It takes a mighty man of valor to raise children in the fear of the Lord.**

A good man leaves an inheritance to his children's children, but the wealth of the sinner is stored up for the righteous (Proverbs 13:22).

For the Lord your God has blessed you in all the work of your hand. He knows your trudging through this great wilderness. These forty years the Lord your God has been with you; you have lacked nothing (Deuteronomy 2:7).

ELIADA—A MIGHTY MAN WHO CAN PROTECT HIS AND OTHERS' INTERESTS

Of Benjamin: Eliada a mighty man of valor, and with him two hundred thousand men armed with bow and shield; and next to him was Jehozabad, and with him one hundred and eighty thousand prepared for war. These served the king, besides those the king put in the fortified cities throughout all Judah (2 Chronicles 17:17–19).

Unlike Jeroboam, the Bible has very little to say about Eliada. From this Scripture we can infer just a few things. We know that he was the youngest of David's sons. He was a descendant of Benjamin. And he was the father of Rezon, an enemy of Solomon. There isn't much other commentary on his background, his childhood, or his career. However, he *was* called a mighty man of valor.

Why was this little-known man labeled as a man of great courage? Eliada knew how to well protect his interests. As captain of the army of Jehoshaphat, he led 200,000 men in war. This mighty man understood the creed of loyalty and how to serve another man faithfully. It is obvious that, because of his military skill, he was designated to govern and train the troops. But there is a deeper element at work here.

It would be far too obvious to commend this man for his courage, being the commando that he was. Although all soldiers are not created equally, they are all expected to display courage because they are soldiers. They are not expected to be fearful, wimpy individuals. I consider all American soldiers—both past and present— to be heroes. Just accepting the challenge of defending our honor, knowing that the possibility exists for dying in the process, shows courage enough for me.

In Eliada's case, I believe that his courage went far beyond his fighting and weaponry skills. I believe that his *heart* was courageous. It takes a courageous heart to defend your interest and to defend your family in the face of imminent death. Far greater than even that, though, is the courage needed to defend another man's interest. This is the kind of courage that Eliada possessed. He did not mind giving his life for another man. That is courage!

In our contemporary society, we are regularly exposed to people who have very little courage for supporting the interest of others. Many men are selfish. They think about themselves and no one else. That is one reason so few men are in our churches today. Many are intimidated by other men, especially by those who possess great strength.

Instead of trying to learn from a mentor, a leader, a businessperson, a pastor, or a professor, far too many men would rather do nothing and reap nothing. You see, it's all about submission. *Submission*—for both men and women—has become a taboo word in our times. Most women believe that submission enslaves their creativity and removes their ability to freely choose for themselves. Too many men see submission as a license to manipulate, control, and even abuse the women whom they claim to love.

> *Wives, submit to your own husbands, as to the Lord. For the husband is head of the wife, as also Christ is head of the church; and He is the Savior of the body. Therefore, just as the church is subject to Christ, so let the wives be to their own husbands in everything* (Ephesians 5:22–24).

What this passage is displaying is a checks and balance system. It is a system of Christian accountability, not slavery. In fact, biblical submission is a beautiful thing because it releases us to be truly free. Wives should be accountable to their husbands. The church is accountable to Christ. Christ represents the husband; the church represents His bride. Only an evil man would mistreat his bride. Any good husband would do everything in his power to please his wife and provide everything that she needed. Christ sets that example for us.

What about the husband? The Bible clearly tells women to submit to their husbands. It instructs the church to be subject to Christ. But, to whom exactly does the man submit? If the man is not submitted to anyone, then why should he expect his wife to submit to him? Obviously, he should not.

The implication is that the man should submit to the Lord. But, how can anyone measure a man's submission to God if he is not saved, if he does not attend church with his wife, or if he totally opposes church altogether? It is very difficult to measure a man's level of submission if he does not submit to someone. Perhaps you've heard some saints say, "I only listen to the Lord." This may sound real spiritual at first, but it actually is rebellion and totally opposes God's order.

It is a Bible study principle that Scripture always agrees with Scripture. So what else does the Bible say? Amos 3:7 says that God always speaks to His prophets. Unless you are Moses, He probably won't speak to you face-to-face. God also sends shepherds after His heart to teach you (see Jeremiah 3:15). It is through these shepherds (pastors) that most men can prove their level of submission. A mighty man of valor will be courageous enough to submit to another man for accountability. For without accountability, every institution will fail—even the institution of marriage.

When a born-again man submits to his pastor, he shows his wife that he has no problem with being accountable. If he can submit, then she can as well. However, if that husband refuses to be accountable, he will always have a difficult time convincing his wife that she should be accountable as well. A wife naturally follows the example that her husband sets for her, whether it is good or bad.

> **A mighty man of valor is courageous enough to submit to another man for accountability.**

The key to enjoying prosperity in all aspects of life—including marriage—is in understanding the law of seedtime and harvest. This law simply states that whatever a man sows, he will reap. It is so simple, yet so powerful. Sow a seed; reap a harvest. Many people have experienced how this law works in the area of finances. But it also works in the area of submission.

How does it work in this case? Well, if you are submitted, then someone will submit to you—possibly your wife and children. *"If you have not been faithful in what is another man's, who will give you what is your own?"* (Luke 16:12) I believe one reason some men suffer from lack is because they first were not faithful in serving the interest of another man. They never sowed in that area. They did not sow submission; now they do not reap submission. Rather, they sowed a wrong attitude, and now they reap *that* harvest.

The worst situation any woman could find herself in is marrying a man who does not understand submission. A man who refuses to submit is potentially abusive and dangerous. He answers to no one. He considers everything he does to be righteous because he has no one in authority to weigh his actions. When a man considers everything he thinks and does to be right, then much of it will be wrong, thus creating a mess. The whole situation can be avoided if, dear brother, you will have the courage of Eliada to simply submit.

> *Every way of a man is right in his own eyes, but the Lord weighs the hearts* (Proverbs 21:2).

Men of courage never shy away from protecting the interest of others and of themselves. Mighty men are not ashamed to admit their loyalty and care for another man and willingly endorse and support his vision. A mighty man of valor will go to any length to protect the posterity and integrity of the one whom he serves. He knows that by doing so he is setting a precedent for others to follow. Furthermore, he knows that such actions are pleasing to the Lord his maker.

> *After David had finished talking with Saul, Jonathan became one in spirit with David, and he loved him as himself. From that day Saul kept David with him and did not let him return to his father's house. And Jonathan made a covenant with David because he loved him as himself* (1 Samuel 18:1–3 NIV)

NAAMAN—A MIGHTY MAN WITH A VISIBLE FAULT

> *Now Naaman, commander of the army of the king of Syria, was a great and honorable man in the eyes of his master, because by him the Lord had given victory to Syria. He was also a mighty man of valor, but a leper* (2 Kings 5:1).

Naaman was a Syrian general held in high honor and esteem by his king. Naaman's fellow countrymen viewed him as their deliverer. He was a mighty warrior and a mighty man of valor.

Although he was a great man, he had a problem: Naaman was a leper. He was afflicted with a disease called white leprosy.

Leprosy is a progressive and highly infectious disease caused by bacterium. This disease attacks the skin, nerves, and flesh. Nodules, bleeding and puss-filled ulcers, white scaly scabs, deformities, and eventually the loss of sensation visibly characterize this disease. And it can be transferred to another person over a long period of close contact. Lepers today have the blessing of highly skilled physicians who are able to treat the disease, but lepers in antiquity had no such fortune.

In biblical times lepers were quarantined away from people. Without any medically known cure, leprosy was fatal. People who contracted the disease were hopeless. Added to that hopelessness was the stigma associated with leprosy. Because leprosy was so contagious, other people acted unusually harshly and uncaring to the disease's victims.

Living with leprosy then was like living with AIDS today. Barring a miracle from God, these sufferers had to live with the dreaded expectation of dying prematurely. However, Naaman did not allow this disease to impede his greatness. He did not allow this affliction to hinder his calling. That quality alone is courageous. Despite the negative stigma surrounding his malady, he knew who he was. Because of his confidence in himself, the people were compelled to view him the same way. This Syrian general simply did not allow his fault to stop him.

What fault, what mistake, or what pitfall can get you to quit? Is it easy for the enemy to discourage your hope for the future by reminding you about your past? You will be a mighty man of valor only when you consistently display the courage to win. No matter what situation confronts you, no matter what losses you face, you must set your face to continue moving forward.

Naaman had a legitimate excuse to quit, to lose heart, to throw in the towel. Instead, he sought out solutions for his healing. One day during a raid, the Syrians captured an Israelite maid who became a servant to Naaman's wife. This girl talked about a Jewish prophet named Elisha who could heal her master. Although Naaman was not an Israelite, he took the risk of faith and believed in the possibility of miraculous healing.

Though the prophet did not appear to Naaman himself, he sent a messenger with the solution. The messenger told Naaman to dip seven times in the filthiest river around—the river Jordan. Being a man a great importance, the general was insulted. If he had to dip in a river, wouldn't the Syrian rivers, the Abana and the Pharpar, be sufficient? Fortunately Naaman's servants convinced him to obey the prophet and in his submission he was miraculously healed.

Naaman had the courage to continue despite his personal affliction. How about you? Every marriage will have flaws. Mistakes are inevitable. Circumstances are not always favorable. But mighty men have courage to continue. They don't quit or split. They use their afflictions and weaknesses as opportunities to climb the ladder toward victory. Mighty men continue to walk even though they have an apparent limp. They cannot be stopped. They do not quit. They are mighty men of valor.

Brother, are you one of these mighty men? C.S. Lewis once said, "Courage is not simply one of the virtues, but the form of every virtue at the testing point." It all comes down to how you view life. Is it a God-given gift? Or is it drudgery? I encourage you to be strong. Be industrious. Be willing to submit. Ignore circumstances. Look at everything that comes your way as an opportunity. Take courage at every point, mighty man of valor!

Chapter Six

Where Are You Going in Life—And Who Are You Taking With You?

He who walks with wise men will be wise, but the companion of fools will be destroyed (Proverbs 13:20).

Before you can settle down with the love of your life in a marriage made in heaven, you must ask yourself a very critical question. *Where am I going in life?* You must answer this question before you dare to invite anyone to join you on your journey. Unfortunately, many people do not have any idea where they really want to go in life. For the most part, people just live one day at a time without setting any real goals or having any genuine aspirations for their lives.

Ask yourself, and be honest in your answer—"Where am I going?" Do it right now.

Were you able to answer the question without hesitation or thinking about it? If you had to stop and think about it, if you couldn't even come up with an answer, then you desperately need to reevaluate your entire life. Not only that, but you also need to reorganize your life. You need to reevaluate your priorities. You need to do more of what is working for you and quit those things that are working against your forward progress. You do not want to waste unnecessary time in life traveling around in aimless circles.

Have you ever noticed that achievers never pour their lives into losers? Achievers intentionally try to connect with people who know where they are going in life. So if you don't know where you are going, you have already reduced your chances of connecting with a person of promise. You appear to others as someone who is lost, who has no direction. And unfortunately, instead of attracting strong achievers, you are garnering interest from the wrong people—those who are waiting for the opportunity to take you in their direction, which is down and out.

HAVING CLEAR-CUT GOALS

What are your dreams and aspirations for the future? Do you have any? I hope you do. I also hope that your dreams and goals are clear-cut. Are they unmistakable—the kind people can automatically know and understand? For instance, when you hear the name Michael Jordan, what immediately comes to your mind? Hopefully it isn't baseball. And I sure hope it isn't gambling.

What most people initially think of is basketball. You might think this example is superfluous, considering that Michael Jordan is the most famous and perhaps the best basketball player in the world. However, did you ever consider that he didn't wake up one morning as a teenager and get all the accolades and praises he gets now?

No, like all other great athletes, artists, entertainers, preachers, and politicians, he had to set goals that would set the pace for where he knew he could go in life. So if someone asks you to marry him, the first question you should ask is, "Where can you take me in life?" If that man stutters at that question, then he is not ready for companionship. Forcing someone into marriage prematurely will only ruin both your life and his.

A man (or a woman) cannot tell you where he is taking you unless he first knows where he is going. If he does not know where he is going, then life will choose his direction for him. It is dangerous to let life make choices for you that you should make yourself. Life sometimes arbitrarily chooses for you such things as poverty, low-income housing, unemployment, depression, loneliness, unexpected sickness, and overall unproductive living. The good news is that you can change all that. You can get a direction and set some goals. Life is far too precious to not be in control.

Write Down Your Goals

Then the Lord answered me and said: "Write the vision and make it plain on tablets, that he may run who reads it. For the vision is yet for an appointed time; but at the end it will speak, and it will not lie. Though it tarries, wait for it; because it will surely come, it will not tarry" (Habakkuk 2:2–3).

Why is it so important that you know where you are going in life and that you set achievable goals? And what does all this have to do with marriage and family? Understanding your direction is the only true way to enjoy total fulfillment in your life and marriage. When you wake up every morning knowing that you have a particular role to perform and that you have a specific purpose in the kingdom of God, you live with a greater sense of value and worth.

You know beyond any doubt that you are making a contribution to life that warrants your being here. Your spouse and family support your work with a great sense of pride, recognizing that you are making a difference in their lives and in the lives of many others. This is directly connected to strong marriages. Perhaps you have heard this saying before: "If you fail to plan, you plan to fail." That statement is so true.

Most people spend more time planning for a dream vacation than they do for their marriage. It may sound a bit facetious, but there are some people who invest more time into detailing their truck or SUV than discovering the details that, once applied, will save their faltering marriages. How does this happen? We fail to write things down and inevitably forget them seconds

> **Understanding your direction is the only true way to enjoy total fufillment in your life and marriage.**

later. It may be all right if you forget the groceries that you meant to purchase. But in marriage missing the little details can be disastrous. You cannot afford to miss the details.

You should have a written plan for your family—a vision for you, your spouse, and your children. It ought to be specific and detailed. We are talking about significant lives here, not scrap metal. You can't expect anyone to follow your plan if there's nothing for people to look at. It would be extremely difficult to build a four-bedroom, two-and-a-half bath, three-car garage home without first having the blueprints. You cannot build without knowing what you want to build or having the blueprints. You won't know what to do or how long it will take.

Writing down your plan for a successful marriage is a primary step toward achieving that success. What should such a plan include? Well, do you want children? Write that down. How many do you want? When do you want them? What goals do you have for each child's life? A college education? Write it all down. Of course, I am not saying that your children will automatically fulfill your every vision for them. They might desire a different career from the one you picked out. But one reason so many children stray so far away is because they have never been given options. They do not know that it is possible or even attainable to achieve more in life.

In other words, if your children see quality options, then even if they don't choose the option of your choice they will be more likely to choose a quality option than not. Say you write down in your plan that, after completing high school, your child will earn an undergraduate degree in political science, then go on to attend Yale law school and graduate with a Juris Doctorate of Law, you may get your desire. The worst case scenario is that your son or daughter will wind up at a community college for a couple of years while he or she sorts out and redirects his or her future plans. At least that child will still be on the right pathway toward success in some area. That's still good.

God Himself employed this method of writing down the things He desired. He desired that His people live lifestyles of holiness and faith. But He did not leave that to chance. He didn't just wish that we would automatically follow the path of righteousness. No, He knew that in order for us to actualize our available options, we would need His Word to remind us of the way we should go. That is why we have the holy Bible.

It is no different with marriage. Your vision for a life together with your spouse should be so clear from your written goals that anyone who reads them should be able to implement your plan of action in their own marriage and cause it so succeed like yours. So write down the expectations you have for a spouse. Write down the steps you will take to make your marriage last for a lifetime. What kinds of things will you do to ensure that your river of love never dries up?

Most marriages begin with fires of passion, but those flames must be fanned in order to keep burning. What will you do to make sure your flame doesn't die down? Temptation will inevitably rise to challenge your faithfulness to each other. It always does. What practical things can you do to guard yourself against yielding to such temptations? How many vacations do you think you need to take to keep your marriage exciting and keep you from getting overwhelmed with life's challenges? How can you and your spouse draw strength from each other when life is at its lowest moments for you?

You need to search out the answers to these and other questions. When you decide on your answers, form a personalized plan that works for you and write it down. In time you will have a list, a manual, a testament, a covenant by which you and your spouse will be bound for life. It really is worth your time and your marriage.

> **What kinds of things will you do to ensure that your river of love never dries up?**

YOU HAVE GOT TO BE *SPECIFIC*

Delight yourself also in the Lord, and He shall give you the desires of your heart. Commit your way to the Lord, trust also in Him, and He shall bring it to pass (Psalm 37:4–5).

And whatever you ask in prayer, you will receive, if you have faith (Matthew 21:22 RSV).

As I was growing up in the Pentecostal church, we young people encountered a kind of underlying idea that God just might send us someone for a spouse who was the ugliest person on earth. The church elders would say, "If the person is saved, filled with the Holy Ghost, and treats you well, then that is all that should matter." I did not buy into that erroneous theology. As a young man, I thought that if God could give me a wife who was saved, Spirit-filled, and treated me right, then she also could be bearable to look at.

Wouldn't it diminish God's ability if you limited Him to only being able to give you second best? God can do anything. He can give you the man or woman of your dreams, not your nightmares. The reason so many fail to receive the spouse of choice is simply because they were not specific. One thing I have realized about the God whom I serve is that He is a God of specifics.

God can give you the man or woman of your dreams, not your nightmares.

God is a God of details. He is a God of accurate design. Everything He does has an order. If you don't believe me, just read Genesis 1. Details really do matter. Now, I will be the first to admit that nothing matters more than the character or the spirit of a person. That is first! You can marry the most outwardly beautiful person in the world yet live in an earthly hell. Who a person is on the inside is of far greater value than a pleasing appearance. However, you *can* have the total package. You can have a spouse with a physically pleasing appearance without having to sacrifice his or her having a pleasant disposition.

So Solomon built the temple and completed it. He lined its interior walls with cedar boards, paneling them from the floor of the temple to the ceiling, and covered the floor of the temple with planks of pine. He partitioned off twenty cubits at the rear of the temple with cedar boards from floor to ceiling to form within the temple an inner sanctuary, the Most Holy Place. The main hall in front of this room was forty cubits long. The inside of the temple was cedar, carved with gourds and open flowers. Everything was cedar; no stone was to be seen. He prepared the inner sanctuary within the temple to set the ark of the covenant of the Lord there. The inner sanctuary was twenty cubits long, twenty wide and twenty high. He overlaid the inside with pure gold, and he also overlaid the altar of cedar (1 Kings 6:14–20 NIV).

The above passage includes just an abridged listing of the details of the temple that Solomon built. You can read more about the description of the temple in 1 Kings 6:14–36 and 2 Chronicles 3:8–17. These passages specifically detail the height, the length, and the width of the structure. They relate the different kinds of wood and building materials used. In fact, certain kinds of wood had to be used for certain doors. All in all, you could say that the builders did not get wholesale discounts on their materials because each section of the temple was specifically designed to meet a need.

Your life is no different. You were made with certain qualities, desires, and needs. That is no reason to feel bad; it is just the way God made you. So you need to have someone in your life who can complement those things. Therefore when you are praying for a mate, you need to ask God, in faith, for the kind of woman or man that you desire. What features are you attracted to? What size of person do you feel most complements you? Do you like darker or more fairly complexioned men or women? Do you want someone who laughs a lot? Or would you like someone who is a deep thinker? Be specific.

God will give you the desire of your heart. But, you have to *specify* what it is you desire. If I were to ask you the make, model, and features of your dream car, you probably could tell me without a moment's hesitation. Can you do the same about a spouse-to-be? Could you describe for me, without a second's pause, the features that are most important to you in a spouse? Or would you say, "Can I get back to you on that?" Most people shy away from specifying those types of details. However, they really do matter.

God will give you the desire of your heart. But, you have to *specify* what it is you desire.

You can be specific in terms of vocation also. What kind of job do you envision your spouse having? Do you dream of marrying a preacher? a professional singer? a golf pro? Perhaps your spouse will own a profitable business before you marry him or her. If you work in education, perhaps you desire your spouse to work in education too. Whatever you desire, God can bring it to pass—if you only believe He will.

Ultimately, you are the one who has to live with the person you choose. You will have to go out in public places and still be proud of your choice. It is you who will have to appreciate how God has made him or her. You also are the one who must love and complement your mate on his or her inward and external attributes. Most of all, you are the one who will commit to love that person forever. Wouldn't it be sensible to ask God to give you your heart's desire?

God will do it. I know, for I asked Him for the woman of my dreams, and I married her. I knew exactly what I wanted her to look like. Although I held jobs in the corporate world, I knew that I was destined to become a full-time pastor and evangelist. Therefore I knew that my wife would have to have the character of a pastor's wife. She would have to be patient and understanding. She would have to instinctively be able to minister to me in ways that only a godly wife could. I was specific, and God gave me exactly what I wanted. If God will do it for me, He will do it for you. The key is this: You have not because you ask not. And when you do ask, be specific!

WHO'S COMING ALONG FOR THE RIDE?

Can just anybody handle where God is taking you? In other words, is your choice of a mate ready spiritually, mentally, and emotionally to support you as you rise to the heights of greatness? Jealousy is a great enemy of your progress. It can totally kill marriages. You need to know exactly whom you are planning to take with you on this journey called life.

Does the person you have in mind fit the criteria that coincide with your vision for life? Can this person provide the necessary support system that is so vital for success? Does he or she love you without reservation? Is he or she willing to stand strong with you in difficult times as well as in promising times? Is this person ready for the success that you have been dreaming of? If not, will he or she ever be ready? You need to know the answers to these questions. You need to know whom you are traveling with.

Not everyone qualifies to travel with you. You and your spouse must have matching ideals. Your value systems must be the same. Both you and your partner must have the desire to go forward in life. You both must have goals. Ultimately, you should view your spouse as a Godsend who will help you to fulfill your purposes in life.

Is your choice of a mate ready spiritually, mentally, and emotionally to support you as you rise to the heights of greatness?

> *But as it is written: "Eye has not seen, nor ear heard, nor have entered into the heart of man the things which God has prepared for those who love Him"* (1 Corinthians 2:9).

If you are an achiever, a person who sets high goals for yourself, and you love God, then you probably already know that you are destined for greatness. As 1 Corinthians 2:9 says, the things that God has prepared for you are beyond human sight and hearing. In other words, God's plans for your life may seem to be so great that you hardly believe them yourself.

The problem is that most of us don't realize how important and sacred God's plans for us actually are. If people don't know where you are going, they can instead take you to the hell they were en route to. You really have to be cautious. Let me give you an illustration that illuminates my point. This is a true story.

There was a young tennis player who was a consummate athlete, winning every tennis championship that he entered. He traveled all around the world competing in matches. He amazed the crowds and wowed the judges. Many people thought that he was the best tennis player since Arthur Ashe. Even as a small child, he had played in junior tennis championships on the national level, winning nearly every meet. His future was clearly marked for greatness. Everyone knew that he was destined to be a professional tennis player with all the fame and fortune that usually follows such a career.

During the summer months he worked hard with his father in the family's painting business. His father owned and operated a painting company that was able to secure lucrative painting contracts with many of the city's low-income housing projects. So for about two months in the summer he worked with his dad to earn extra spending money for his trips with his tennis team.

While working in the city's more rundown housing projects, he met a woman who had moved from a different state in a desperate attempt to escape her abusive past. She had been abused as a child, and as she reached adulthood she could not seem to find a man who would not abuse her.

One day while this young tennis star was painting in the hallway of the unit, he happened to notice a man repeatedly hitting this young woman in the face and stomach. His manly protective instinct prompted him to help her. He bravely challenged the man to fight him instead. Since the abuser really was a coward, he immediately ran off and was never seen again. This act of bravery really impressed the battered woman.

A relationship began. Now, this young man did not know anything about the woman or her past. Had he known, I'm sure he would have run away from her with the same fear that her abuser had run from him. As the summer passed, he spent more and more time with her. They became sexually intimate. He talked less and less about playing tennis. He dropped off the team, stopped practicing, and began drinking heavily. He totally lost sight of the vision he once had to be a tennis star. Eventually she got pregnant, they lived together for about seven years, then—against his family's wishes and warnings—he married her.

This woman had had one child prior to meeting him; now together they have eight children. From the day that he met her, his finances have been devastated. They have lived poorly from the very start until now. This woman uses the fact that she has so many children as an excuse and a reason for why people need to give them money, furniture, clothing, vehicles, and food. She shamelessly begs from anybody whom she believes can support her.

Unfortunately, for him it has become a total embarrassment to live with such a woman. He chooses to stay in the marriage not so much for love but because he is too embarrassed to admit to his family that he was wrong.

Not one day during their long time together has she ever encouraged him to pursue his dreams. Her low self-esteem caused her to believe that if he pursued his dreams of playing tennis, she would be neglected in the process. His whole life became one dwindling defeat after another—all because he married someone who was not compatible with him. He married a woman who needed far more help than he could provide. Fixing her situation was a job that only God could perform.

She was a hurting woman seeking to hurt a man. Now, she wasn't doing this on purpose. She wasn't trying to hurt someone else because of an inborn evil nature. Rather, it was a response to her internal pain. It was a defense mechanism. But it destroyed him.

This very day they live in horrible poverty. Three times this husband nearly overdosed on unusually high amounts of alcohol. The Department of Children and Families has threatened to remove their children for child neglect and for allowing them to live in an area unfit for human occupancy. Still their situation has not changed.

Now in his mid-forties, you can often find this former tennis star sitting on a park bench or in his car totally stoned from drinking. You may know that when people are drunk, they speak their truest heart. If you were to walk up to this man while he is in this condition, you may hear him say things such as, "I could have been the world's greatest tennis player if only...." It is obvious yet unfortunate that this man totally missed his opportunity in life. He lost it because of who he chose to take along with him in life.

No matter how often you connect a great asset to a total liability, the liability always wins. You have to consider whom you connect with. Your future spouse should have the ability and willingness to support your efforts and help you become the absolute best in life. Anybody can be company. But you don't need mere company. If you need companionship, get a pet. What you need is someone to help you fulfill your purposes in God. That someone should enhance you and make you better and more effective.

This ride lasts for life. Make sure you know who is on the marriage ride. It is absolutely crucial to your development in life.

Chapter Seven

Why Get Married Anyway?

Dr. Myles Munroe often says, "Where purpose is not known, abuse is inevitable." He then adds that there is a purpose for everything that is created. So I have a question for you. "Who created marriage?" If you answered "God," you answered correctly. God is the Creator and founder of the institution of marriage. Now, let me ask you another question. "Do you know why marriage exists?" Before you get married, you must know why (the reason and goal) you're getting married.

Some people get married because, absurdly, they think it is the "in" thing to do. Their best friend got married, so now they want to exchange lifelong vows too. Others get married because they are lonely and falsely believe that marriage will help to fill their void. That kind of marriage usually makes both parties miserable. If you are not happy—and I mean extremely happy—as a single person, then you will never be happily married.

You should not make marriage the basis of your happiness. If you are looking for marriage to fill your missing sense of joy, you may wait for a lifetime. However, if you are already complete and full of happiness as a single, then you can add your spirit of joy and wholeness to that spirit in someone else. But don't get married expecting your spouse to fill voids that only God can fill. Not only is such pressure on them totally unrealistic, but also grossly unfair.

Still others get married because they view it as a legal avenue to get all the sex they have been dreaming of having. I have some news for you. Many couples, after they consummate the marriage and live together for a while, don't find sex as inviting as it was in the beginning. Other priorities begin to supersede the few moments of sexual pleasure—such as working to pay the mortgage and properly rearing the children.

People choose to marry for far more reasons than I have the time to list. But one thing is for sure. If you don't know anything about marriage, first get a grip on why it exists before you enter into it. It is not an institution to be entered into lightly.

It is not a light thing to exchange covenantal vows. Marriage requires fortitude to hold on tightly when the winds of life begin to blow. Many divorces could have been averted if only people had thought first before making what God considers to be a lifetime decision.

If you don't know anything about marriage, first get a grip on why it exists before you enter into it.

Why does marriage exist in the first place? If you are already married, the answer may make you want to refashion your marriage after this model. It may make you reconsider your decision to get married. Or you may still choose to pursue this covenant relationship. Whichever you choose, know that you took the thoughtful, informed course.

THE PURPOSE OF MARRIAGE

Many theologians and students of the Bible over the years have tried to discover exactly why God created marriage. Of the many suggestions they present, one of the most common ones deals with sex. "God created marriage just for sex," they say. I disagree. Although God designed sexual expression to be within the boundaries of marriage, sex is not the reason for which marriage was created. (I will deal more with this topic of sex in the next chapter.)

Others say God created marriage as the basis for procreation. I realize that children best fulfill their optimum potential when raised within the confines of marriage. When both mother and father are in the home, a child is more likely to enjoy the solid, spiritual infrastructure needed to raise godly children. The Bible even lets us know that the power of two has a greater ability of effectuating change than just one.

Two are better than one, because they have a good reward for their labor. For if they fall, one will lift up his companion. But woe to him who is alone when he falls, for he has no one to help him up. Again, if two lie down together, they will keep warm; but how can one be warm alone? (Ecclesiastes 4:9–11, emphasis added).

Again I say to you, that ***if two of you agree on earth about anything*** *that they may ask,* ***it shall be done*** *for them by My Father who is in heaven. For where two or three have gathered together in My name, I am there in their midst* (Matthew 18:19–20 NAS, emphasis added).

Although God does not condone conceiving children out of wedlock, He does not throw away the child. Regardless of how irresponsible a parent may have been in his or her premature decisions to conceive children without first counting the cost, the child is still precious and valuable in the eyes of the Lord. The Bible records the lives of several people born out of wedlock yet who still became great. How they were born was not as important as how they chose to live. Naturally, it matters the most if people choose to live for God.

So that takes care of that idea. Having children is not the principle reason God created marriage. Children are a by-product of marriage and a symbol of the fruitfulness of the union, not the reason for its creation. Sex is not the reason either. If it were, then sex alone could sustain a marriage. I have yet to meet anyone whose marriage endured just because of sex. So why did God create marriage?

I believe that the purpose of marriage is threefold, like God Himself is threefold. First, marriage *forms a unit*. Second, it allows a couple to *acquire wealth*. Third, it *provides security for generations*.

Marriage forms a unit

The first reason God created marriage is *to form a unit*. The Bible says in Matthew 19:6, *"They are no longer two but one flesh."* You are no longer two people, but rather one couple. You are one in your vision and purpose in life. You are one in your love for the Lord and your desire to promote His kingdom.

In a practical sense you have given up your right to use the word *mine* forever. In a godly marriage the new word becomes *ours*. It is no longer my bed but rather our bed. It is no longer my car but our car. Although the man may have used his money to purchase the house, the house belongs to the both of you. Trying to keep things your own in a marriage will always breed great struggles.

Accept the truth that you are one. The two of you have become fused together. And, like fine wine, you get better and more valuable over time. Much like the precious stones that are given in an engagement ring, the marriage becomes increasingly valuable after it lasts through the process of pressurization and the application of intense fire.

So God's goal for your marriage is the same goal Jesus has for His body, called the church: that they might be one. (Read John 17.) This goal alone best symbolizes the very reason marriage should exist—to become one. That is why it is so very important to not become unequally yoked with an unbeliever.

When yoked together, an unbeliever and a believer will always be at odds with one another. They serve totally different gods. On the other hand, when two people who both love God and support His purpose come together in holy matrimony, they become one in spite of their diverse cultures and varying backgrounds. In the kingdom of God, in the church at large, and in marriage, Jesus desires us to be one.

> *Now I am no longer in the world, but these are in the world, and I come to You. Holy Father, keep through Your name those whom You have given Me, that they may be one as We are* (John 17:11).

Marriage allows you to acquire wealth

The second purpose of marriage is *to acquire wealth*. You should not acquire wealth simply to hoard it for yourself. Yes, acquiring wealth is the foundation for you to establish yourself in life. It also is so that you can well take care of the needs of your family. You should never need the assistance of state welfare, which in its simplest form is a type of slavery. The Bible says, *"But if anyone does not provide for his own, and especially for those of his household, he has denied the faith and is worse than an unbeliever"* (1 Timothy 5:8).

If you have wealth, then you are not forced to become a slave to the social welfare system. With wealth you can pick and choose those things that you desire. The moment you get married (and maybe even before), you should be looking to buy property. Don't settle for an apartment for the rest of your life. You are only making someone else rich. And you shouldn't even think about living with your mother.

The man who doesn't have a place to put his wife should not even think about marriage. He is not ready for marriage if he has to bring you back home to Momma. Brother, God made women and men different. We have very different needs. A woman has a deep emotional need to feel secure, and she cannot feel secure when she is living in another woman's house.

If you are living in this kind of a situation, don't get discouraged. Just hurry up and get out of it to save your marriage. The point is, when you have wealth, you won't have to live in a compromising situation because you will have options to choose from.

You also should consider starting a business. Face it, in the system that we live in here in America, it is nearly impossible to acquire wealth from a weekly salary. At best you can pay your bills working a nine-to-five job. For the most part you are living life paycheck to paycheck. This is not God's best for you or your family. You need to ask God to give you a business idea. Ask Him to show you what is not being done in your area. Find a need and fill it. If you do that, you will have more wealth than you would ever imagine.

As a final note, you and your family should want to advance the kingdom of God in this earth. As a family unit you simply cannot do that until you get wealth. It requires money to support foreign missions, to build churches, and to win souls to Christ. The more wealth you have, the more you will be able to make a difference in the kingdom of God. After all, it is God who gives us the power to acquire wealth. He does not have any problem with us using that wealth as long as it does not use us.

> And you shall remember the Lord your God, for it is He who gives you power to get wealth, that He may establish His covenant which He swore to your fathers, as it is this day (Deuteronomy 8:18).

Marriage secures the generations

This leads us to the third purpose, which is *to leave an inheritance for your children's children*. *"A good man leaves an inheritance for his children's children, but a sinner's wealth is stored up for the righteous"* (Proverbs 13:22 NIV). The Bible clearly identifies a distinguishing characteristic of a good or a righteous man. He leaves an inheritance for his children and his grandchildren.

How many men do you know who, when they died, left an inheritance for their children? I am not talking about a five thousand dollar insurance policy. I mean they left such a substantial amount of money that their family members were free from financial worries and concerns forever. Most people don't reach this level in life. On the contrary, too many people leave financial debts and other burdens for their children when they die. *This is not the will of God.*

One reason you should live life with an inheritance mind-set is so the next generations will be free from having to chase the dollar in order to live. Children should be born into modern-day dynasties and Spirit-filled legacies in which they are fully provided for from the day they are born. The very day your son or daughter is born, you should already have made plans for how his secondary education, college expenses, and wedding plans will be paid for.

Long before you finally rest, you should have already determined what you desire to leave your family with to ensure that they will be well taken care of after you are gone. I know most people don't like to talk about these kinds of things, but they are reality. Far too many people in the world—perhaps billions—cannot do anything to help their children prosper in life. That is extremely sad.

Children should be born into modern-day dynasties and Spirit-filled legacies in which they are fully provided for from the day they are born.

If you cannot provide the help that your children need, they will inevitably be forced to seek out worldly methods to sustain them. You should never put your family in this position. You will know they won't only when you choose to live with an inheritance mind-set.

CHECK YOUR MOTIVATION

Now that you know the purpose for marriage, check your motivation. Why do you want to get married? Are you taking this step for selfish reasons? Do you really love the person whom you are about to vow to marry? Are you willing to go through the tough process that makes marriages strong and valuable? Or do you have a time limit on how long you expect to be in the marriage? When you answer these questions truthfully and honestly, they will lead you to your heart's true motive.

Some men marry a pretty face as if that face was a trophy to be showcased in public. Deep down this man does not really love his wife. His motive was wrong. He married for the wrong reasons. Sooner or later those reasons are going to backfire. You should marry primarily because you have a strong desire to become one with the person whom you are married to.

More times than I care to remember I've seen a woman get married because she is pregnant and a man get married because that woman is carrying his child. As we've touched on before, this may seem like a great reason to marry, but it too is motivated wrongly. So many marriages that began this way fail. Just because you are pregnant or you got someone pregnant does not mean that that person should become your spouse. There is far more to marriage than having someone's baby.

Sometimes women trap men by conceiving a child in an attempt to keep the man with her forever. Obviously that is a wrong motive. Not only is it unfair to each other, but it also is unfair to the child. Usually people believe that it's better for this child if both parties got married, but that still doesn't work. Only when love is a couple's motivation for being together will the marriage have a good basis.

In the many cases I've seen in which two people get married for the sake of a child, both parents nearly hate each other. They fight all the time and cannot seem to get along. Such a contentious relationship is not one that any child should be born into! Just because you messed up once does not mean that you have to continue to mess up. Entering into marriage out of pity or in an effort to right a wrong will only cause you more grief in the long run.

Only when love is a couple's motivation for being together will the marriage have a good basis.

Love should be your guide at all times. I suggest that every person, whether married, unmarried, or intending to be married, should read and meditate on 1 Corinthians 13, a passage known as the love chapter. This chapter conveys the true motive of love so strongly that I am including it here. Read these verses over and over again until they become a natural part of your character and spirit.

Though I speak with the tongues of men and of angels, but have not love, I have become sounding brass or a clanging cymbal. And though I have the gift of prophecy, and understand all mysteries and all knowledge, and though I have all faith, so that I could remove mountains, but have not love, I am nothing. And though I bestow all my goods to feed the poor, and though I give my body to be burned, but have not love, it profits me nothing. Love suffers long and is kind; love does not envy; love does not parade itself, is not puffed up; does not behave rudely, does not seek its own, is not provoked, thinks no evil; does not rejoice in iniquity, but rejoices in the truth; bears all things, believes all things, hopes all things, endures all things. Love never fails. But whether there are prophecies, they will fail; whether there are tongues, they will cease; whether there is knowledge, it will vanish away. For we know in part and we prophesy in part. But when that which is perfect has come, then that which is in part will be done away. When I was a child, I spoke as a child, I understood as a child, I thought as a child; but when I became a man, I put away childish things. For now we see in a mirror, dimly, but then face to face. Now I know in part, but then I shall know just as I also am known. And now abide faith, hope, love, these three; but the greatest of these is love (1 Corinthians 13).

IS IT BETTER TO REMAIN SINGLE?

Because of the present crisis, I think that it is good for you to remain as you are. Are you married? Do not seek a divorce. Are you unmarried? Do not look for a wife. But if you do marry, you have not sinned; and if a virgin marries, she has not sinned. But those who marry will face many troubles in this life, and I want to spare you this (1 Corinthians 7:26–28 NIV).

This passage almost seems like a grim warning from the apostle Paul not to get married. Did Paul have an aversion toward marriage? What exactly did he mean? Look closer at these verses. The first reason Paul said that it is better to be alone is because of *"the present crisis."* More than likely he was referring to the hostile way Christians were being treated and to the persecutions that they were subjected to at that time.

Christians in that day and age were beaten literally to death. They were imprisoned for declaring the name of Jesus. Unfathomable atrocities were perpetrated against the saints. Those were very difficult times to live in if you confessed Jesus Christ as your Lord. It was much like the pressures that a Middle Eastern person today faces when he or she decides to abandon the Islamic faith. The persecution was great. So Paul's logic was that it was better to not be married, to be alone, rather than to draw a spouse into the crisis as well. "Let her be alone," he was saying. "She will be better off that way."

Another reason Paul might have suggested staying single was because of his own calling. Paul had a great destiny, and often people who have a sense of destiny upon their lives can see the destiny in the lives of others. Paul was called to preach Jesus to the Gentiles. That was his entire mission. So he saw time as being short. As a result, it wouldn't make sense to marry. Not if Jesus was coming soon.

Perhaps Paul misinterpreted a sensing in his spirit of his own imminent death with the second coming of the Lord. Then it would make the best sense to stay single, especially if a couple could not share real quality time with one another anyhow.

The third possible reason Paul suggested that a person stay single is by far the best of the three and the one most applicable to our modern day saints.

> But I want you to be without care. He who is unmarried cares for the things of the Lord—how he may please the Lord. But he who is married cares about the things of the world—how he may please his wife (1 Corinthians 7:32–33).

A single man or woman can wholly devote him or herself to the purposes of the Lord without any hindrances. It's just a fact of life. Although I will call upon various ministers within our church to perform needed functions, I fully realize that the single ministers have a greater ability to serve our church to the fullest without interruption. If I have need of one of my married ministers at three o' clock in the morning, they will probably be there for me, but it would be grossly inconsiderate to his wife and family.

A husband's first obligation is to minister to his family. God knows this, for He is the one who established this order. Once you become married, your involvement in other areas decreases. It may not decrease drastically, but it will decrease. And that is to be expected. However, the single person does not have a spouse to answer to. He or she has the right to make the sole judgment on how, when, and where he or she can serve.

If you are single and you can live a celibate life without a struggle, then you should remain single. Your gift of singleness will be a tremendous unmatched blessing to the kingdom of God. However, if you do not possess the grace of celibacy—and not everybody does—then it is good that you should marry. It may not seem like it, but Paul was *not* putting a guilt trip on the people who desired to be married. Marriage is honorable, and if you have been successful and whole during your single life, then it is totally fine for you to join with another whole person in marriage.

MAKING A DIFFERENCE IN LIFE

More than anything else, I hope that you will view yourself, your spouse, and your family as people who are on this earth to make a difference in life. Think about it. Why are you here? Why is your spouse here? What on earth do you want to bring children into this world for? I trust that you have an intense desire to change the world. In light of the turbulent times in which we live, God desires people who will live their lives intentionally trying to make a difference.

That should be your goal. Through your life and your Christian witness you need to make it known that you are on this earth to make it better. You should make it your aim that when you die, you will leave this earth a better place. Jesus Himself commanded us to be a light in a world shrouded with darkness. Unfortunately, we often lose sight of that mandate. You really can help to make this world a better place—but it starts with you.

> *You are the light of the world. A city that is set on a hill cannot be hidden. Nor do they light a lamp and put it under a basket, but on a lampstand, and it gives light to all who are in the house. Let your light so shine before men, that they may see your good works and glorify your Father in heaven* (Matthew 5:14–16).

Chapter Eight

Thou Shalt Not Burn—Understanding Sex in Marriage

*But I say to the unmarried and to the widows: It is good for
them if they remain even as I am; but if they cannot exercise
self-control, let them marry. For it is better to marry than to
burn with passion* (1 Corinthians 7:8–9).

As a child growing up in the church, I would hear the older
pastors and often the mothers of the church tell the younger folks
that it was better to marry than to burn. Some of the pastors then
were not really all that well learned; they took stabs at defining the
Scriptures rather than properly dividing the Word. They would
say that 1 Corinthians 7:9 meant that it was better to marry someone whom you had passion for rather than to burn in hell. Now, as
an adult, I realize that this Scripture was not saying that at all.

At that time I couldn't determine whether what they said was
actually true or not. So like most kids and probably most adults we
just accepted what they told us as truth, without asking any further
questions. We were taught to be submissive to authority no matter
what. Although I believe in being submitted to authority (see Ro-
mans 13), I do not see anything wrong with asking questions to get
a clarification of something that is difficult to understand.

*Wisdom is the principal thing; therefore get wisdom. And in
all your getting, get understanding* (Proverbs 4:7).

Many things about sexuality I just didn't understand as a
young person. As I grew up I began to realize there were many
unanswered questions that the church at large simply would not
provide answers for. I am sure their heart motive was genuine.
However, those within the church were a bit uncomfortable talking

about the human sexual experience. For some reason they seemed to get embarrassed every time the subject came up.

Instead of dealing with the topic head-on, the church leaders would get deeply spiritual and start reciting all the scriptural prohibitions concerning fornication and adultery. It is true that the Bible is very clear about sexual sin and the consequences it carries. And that discussion needed to be very open and forthright with the youth and young people. Yet, the other aspects of sex—the godly aspects, if you will—were never even broached.

In today's over-sexed society, it might be beneficial to inform even children about the righteous order of sex. To leave such instruction in the hands of our public educational system is very unwise, and may be even worse than their learning it on the streets. Because so many people hate to deal with the truth about this real issue, we're tackling it head-on in this chapter!

Let's be honest. Sex has been around since the beginning of humankind. It is how you and I arrived on the scene. And it is not going anywhere. Whether you like it or not, sex is here to stay. However, there are proper and improper approaches toward sex. We're going to look at both. It's time we examine the real deal about this much avoided area.

THE REAL LOWDOWN ON SEX

It is very unfortunate that we (the church) have allowed secular society not only to define sex, but also to diminish it to the point where many Christians no longer believe sexual expression to be a beautiful, God-ordered act. Church folks have accepted sex as being nasty. Even married folks are ashamed to talk about sex freely, like it is some sort of taboo subject. In fact, through years of counseling people—both married and unmarried—I have discovered that married couples tend to have less sex than unmarried people. This just should not be.

It is a sad fact that some married couples have allowed the spirit of familiarity to diminish their spouse's value in their eyes. Husbands no longer view their wife as the queen she *is*—or should I say "was?" Wives no longer view their husband as the lovemaking machine and prince they once saw him as. Sex after marriage tends to become boring and lifeless, to say the least. What happened to cause this breakdown?

Here is my answer. When you (the married person) allow yourself to see sex as anything other than a beautiful expression that is God-given and God-ordained, you have devalued the whole process. You should never say, "I remember when it used to be good...." *In the confines of marriage, sex should always be good.* Isn't it interesting that unsaved people who are unmarried will confess, tell stories, and reenact their wonderful sexual fantasies without shame or reservation?

They do not have God's consent to indulge in such pleasures, yet they do it without heaven's permission and enjoy it. It is a work of Satan for single people to have a greater joy and excitement about sex than married people. Unfortunately, that is just the way things are. But the real truth is this: God designed sex. It was God's idea, not man's.

Neither did God create sex for the sole purpose of procreation. I have read about different religious sects in which wives have sex with their husbands only for the sake of getting pregnant and bearing children. Some barbaric cultures even sever the woman's genitalia to make sure she can't "catch a feeling."

> **In the confines of marriage, sex should always be good.**

That is cruel and unusual torture! It also perpetuates an unethical message, one that I believe has become a part of many Christian orders. That message says sex should not be pleasurable. Why do people hide the truth that sex should be an extremely pleasurable experience? Within the confines of marriage it should be an encounter unparalleled by any other in the human experience. The only way people will ever believe it is if married couples begin to confess how good sex in marriage actually is.

If sex in marriage appears to be boring, then the enemy will creep in and sow seeds of lustful thoughts. He will embellish and overdramatize what sex would be like with someone other than your spouse. It is all a trick of the devil to steal your loved ones, kill your influence, and destroy the family unit as God designed it to be. You must be wiser than the crowd that chooses to go down the road that leads to death and destruction.

> *To deliver you from the immoral woman, from the seductress who flatters with her words, who forsakes the companion of her youth, and forgets the covenant of her God. For her house leads down to death, and her paths to the dead; none who go to her return, nor do they regain the paths of life* (Proverbs 2:16–19).

SEX *IS* GOOD

> *Marriage is honorable among all, and the bed undefiled; but fornicators and adulterers God will judge* (Hebrews 13:4).

When you get married (if you are already married, you can do this now), you need to make a regular confession—particularly to your spouse—that sex is good. Don't be shy about it. Go ahead and say it out loud. If you are married to the love of your life, then this confession should be easy to repeat over and again. Keep in mind that love is always centered in the will, not the emotions. Love is a choice. Lovemaking is also a choice. And your response to that lovemaking is a choice.

You can choose to enjoy it, or you can decide to hate it. It really is that simple. Your choice will depend greatly upon how you sincerely feel about your spouse. And how you feel about your spouse depends greatly on what you say. I encourage the young married men in my church to say nice things to their wives. I tell them to compliment her dress, her hairstyle, the way she looks, and the way she walks.

I try to get the men to notice the things that can easily be overlooked, like the small broach that she may wear from time to time. Brother, compliment your wife on the new fragrance she is wearing. Women, you should do the same. Confess how wonderfully handsome your man is. Let him know that he is smart and exercises the type of mental genius that turns you on. "But what if my husband is not so smart?" you may ask.

Find something that he does well and compliment it. Maybe it's how he faithfully takes out the trash. Perhaps he mows the lawn with a spirit of excellence. Maybe he can cook a mean steak. I don't know—but I'm sure you do. The point is, you need to take the time to try and discover what his good points are and then affirm him with your words. I can guarantee that when you begin to use your words to create an environment of romance, you will begin to see major changes in your love life.

Only a fool wants to be insulted, humiliated, and talked down to. You don't like those feelings, and neither does your spouse. The more positive affirmation you can give and receive from each other, the more quickly you will create a loving climate rather than a hostile environment.

You may now ask, "But what if the sex is not good at all?" If the sex is not to your liking, then you need to let your spouse know. Open up your mouth and voice what changes you believe will make a difference. Your mate won't know unless you say something. Communication is needed in the bedroom as well.

When you begin to use your words to create an environment of romance, you will begin to see major changes in your love life.

Get in the habit of using your words to build each other up. There are more than enough people in the world who do just the opposite.

THE POWER OF CREATION AND CREATIVITY

In the beginning God created the heavens and the earth (Genesis 1:1).

One way you can keep your sexual life active is to become more creative. Boredom runs rampant in the land. Our society is always looking for something new and exciting to spark our interest. Anything that is old becomes less useful than when it was brand-new. If nothing else, you can make a difference in your love life just by choosing different words. Words pack a creative force. God Himself used words to create the heavens and the earth.

If God can create an entire universe with His words, isn't it just possible then that you can change your marriage, your love life, and your passion with words too? I know you can. God is a creator, and so are you. We are created in His image! But you must *be* creative in order to *create*. Some people add richness to the world by their *creativity*—songwriters, authors, poets, artists, photographers, etc.

On the technical side of things, these creative wonders design computer programs, architectural drawings, and blueprints for bridges and monumental structures. What all of these creative people have in common is a desire to express themselves through their gifting in a way that the world has never seen or experienced before. In the same way, married people should not view sex in the same way they look at the old painting that has been on the wall for eighty-five years. It is time to take that painting down and put up a new one.

Both the man and the woman have to become freer and more creative when they come together to make love. Husband, ask your wife what she likes. Wife, ask your husband what turns him on. Ask each other questions that reveal what you desire. Find your spouse's need and fill it. Not everyone is alike. Each individual has different needs. What one likes, the other might totally hate. Be considerate, but don't be afraid to try! Need I be any more plain?

If I want to know what my wife likes, I ask her. There's no shame in that. The marriage bed is undefiled, the Scriptures say. It is your private showroom. It is the place where you can be as creative as you desire to be. Take the brakes off. Quit making love the way your grandparents did and enjoy the gift of God in each other. God created you to create. The possibilities are endless. The sky is the limit.

WHOSE SPIRIT ARE YOU ALLOWING TO ENTER?

Did you know that every time you have sex with a person, a transfer of spirits takes place? That fact alone means you must not take the issue of sex lightly. If sexually transmitted diseases were the only reason to abstain from sex before marriage, that would be enough. But when you add potential defilement from the spirits attached to your partner, it pushes it to a whole new level. So not only can you possibly catch a disease and die, but you also can end up living with another person's spiritual oppression (unless you wash away that spiritual defilement with the blood of Jesus).

When you have sex, a physical *and* a spiritual exchange take place. Have you ever heard the phrase, "sleeping with the enemy"? It is not just the title of a movie. It can be a reality. Many times people do not realize just how much they have been affected by sleeping with someone illicitly until after the fact.

If you claim to be born again and yet you become physically intimate with someone who does not love the Lord, it will have a drastic effect on your life. Slowly you will regress. Your love for God will diminish over time. Why? You will have allowed someone you do not know to enter into your course. That's why sex is called intercourse.

> When you have sex, a physical *and* a spiritual exchange take place.

Intercourse—entering your course. You can't allow anyone to fill the place that God has reserved for your marriage partner. Be careful, be holy, and be wise.

DON'T USE YOUR BODY TO CONTROL

The Bible defines witchcraft as divination, which deals with acquiring secret knowledge—especially knowledge that is related to the future. It deals with evoking spirits of dead people. Witchcraft also goes into the art of performing magic and casting spells. But in its broadest sense, witchcraft is simply what a familiar spirit uses to control and manipulate its victims.

To most children and many adults, witches are fairy-tale characters that ride brooms. That image is simply a smoke screen of the enemy. Witchcraft is practiced much closer to you than you may realize. For many married men, witchcraft is taking place each night in their bedroom. Allow me to explain.

Over the years I have been a pastor, I have counseled countless couples of whom the husband confessed to me that his wife refuses to make love to him. As always when I hear statements like these, I ask questions. "Has your husband been unfaithful to you? Has he been verbally, emotionally, or physically abusive toward you or your children? Do you feel that you are in a life-threatening situation by living with this man?" Any one of those scenarios would make anyone with good sense shut down sexually. However, the wife usually answers with a confident "no" to all my questions.

I then ask her, "Why are you not making love to your husband?" Some of the answers I hear are simply unbelievable. Here's a short list of some of them. "I am growing apart from him…He did not do what I wanted him to do for me…He did not buy me what I asked him to…If he does not do what I tell him to do, then he just won't get any…There is more to life than sex…I just don't feel like having sex anymore…I am not attracted to him like that…I don't want him on me…I spend all my quality time meditating on the Word of God. Surely that's more important than sex."

None of those answers are legitimate reasons for withholding sex! The bottom line is, if you are using sex to manipulate your spouse, then you are succumbing to a spirit of control, and that leads to witchcraft. As a Christian woman, it should be your highest goal to please God and to help your husband fulfill his purposes in God.

Now, to be balanced, I am not saying that if your husband is abusive or unfaithful that you are obligated to risk your health by allowing him to have sex with you. That would not be responsible behavior. But if he has *not* committed an offense against you, and you choose to use your body as a way to control, then you are not using your body in the manner that God designed.

Your body was not intended or designed as a tool to manipulate others into giving you everything that you beg for. That is not why God created sex. When you are married, your body belongs to your husband and his body belongs to you. That means sex should be something you mutually agree on, something that works in favor of both parties, not just one. Since God's Word is the final court of appeal, let's look at what the Bible has to say about the whole matter.

> *Now concerning the things of which you wrote to me: It is good for a man not to touch a woman. Nevertheless, because of sexual immorality, let each man have his own wife, and let each woman have her own husband. Let the husband render to his wife the affection due her, and likewise also the wife to her husband. The wife does not have authority over her own body, but the husband does. And likewise the husband does not have authority over his own body, but the wife does. Do not deprive one another except with consent for a time, that you may give yourselves to fasting and prayer; and come together again so that Satan does not tempt you because of your lack of self-control* (1 Corinthians 7:1–5).

Here again Paul offered the single person a proposal. He told them that it was good for a man not to touch a woman. Remember, the Word agrees with the Word, so this verse does not contradict God's heart toward Adam when he was alone. *"And the Lord God said, 'It is not good that man should be alone; I will make him a helper comparable to him'"* (Genesis 2:18). Paul's point was that if a man does not touch a woman, he will not have the feelings and emotions connected with having touched a woman.

In other words, if a man has never experienced that level of intimacy, then it should not distract him from doing the will of God to the maximum when called upon. Sexual sins had become far too common in the Corinthian church. To correct the problem, Paul informed every man to have his own wife in order to satisfy his sexual needs. Likewise, every woman was to have her own husband to fulfill her sexual desire.

Then Paul wrote that the wife should allow her husband to make love to her when he has the need, and vice versa. It works both ways. He explained that when a person is married, he or she gives up the right to say "no." Marriage binds a person body, soul, and spirit to the spouse. Then the apostle warned that if one partner does not consent to minister to the other's sexual needs, the other partner may be tempted to engage in an illicit sexual act. His or her sexual desire might get out of hand. Now, this does not mean that individual is not held accountable for his or her wanton behavior. But the entire thing could have been avoided if godly wisdom were applied.

Therefore, according to this Scripture, if a wife withholds her body from her husband, she causes him to be tempted by Satan, the founder of witchcraft. Neither the man nor the woman has a right to deprive the other of sex unless it is for a short time of prayer, fasting, and spiritual consecration. And even under those conditions both parties must be in full agreement.

If you are manipulating your spouse in this manner, using your body to control him or her, repent right now, in the name of Jesus. Decide to change. Ask God to forgive you for allowing yourself to be used by the enemy. Sex is not supposed to be a lopsided issue. Both parties should be mutually fulfilled and satisfied. Neither person should feel taken advantage of or unfulfilled. When that happens, the whole act becomes most unpleasant. Allow sex to become the win-win situation God intended it be.

Therefore if the Son makes you free, you shall be free indeed (John 8:36).

COMMUNICATION—THE KEY TO LASTING MARRIAGES AND GREAT SEX

I purposely have saved the best for last. Communication is the key to lasting marriages. Good communication in marriage accounts for more than eighty percent of the marriage itself. Finances play a role, as does sex, but in much smaller capacities than communication. Many men don't realize that if the communication aspect isn't going all that well, then the sex won't be all that great either. They sort of go hand in hand. Great communication equals great lovemaking. Horrible communication, fighting, bickering, complaining, and confusion equals _____ . You fill in the blank!

Although lovemaking is important, your exchange of words each day far outweighs one night of thick passion. Dr. Stephen Covey, author of the best-selling book, *The 7 Habits of Highly Effective People*, says that you should first seek to understand, not to be understood. That is a power-filled statement. Most people do just the opposite.

We always want to be heard, understood, and felt. Perhaps that is why there are so many splits. I'm sure you have seen examples of this. Two people go into business together as partners. Yet, down the road they can't seem to see eye to eye on an issue. Instead of reasoning together, they foolishly dissolve the partnership, losing the dream both worked so hard to achieve. What folly!

Communication is the key to lasting marriages.

Communication is everything. Communication is the breath that gives life to any relationship—especially the marriage relationship. Without healthy communication your relationship is bound to die. "What actually is communication, and how does it work?" I'm glad you asked. The first thing you must realize is that communication does not mean a whole bunch of talking. Neither does it mean that a person is always heard.

Communication is like a two-way street. One person listens while the other person talks. Although verbal communication is the most common form, it is not the only way to communicate. You can communicate non-verbally through gestures and body language. Your facial expression can communicate messages. (Haven't you ever winked at your loved one from across the room?) The highest level of communication occurs, however, when you don't have to say anything and yet the other person knows exactly what is being communicated.

As Dr. Covey told us, our highest aim should not be communicating our feelings, our goals, our intentions, and our aspirations, but rather hearing the other person's. We should seek and desire to understand another person's point of view. In marriage, when you place your spouse's feelings and concerns above yours, you will always enjoy mountaintop experiences during lovemaking.

Many marriage advocates teach that finances are the main reason for marital separation and divorce. Although money is a real issue and bears a great weight on a marriage, it alone does not matter most. Communication still far outweighs financial matters. If couples would communicate more, then unnecessary and unregulated spending would never happen. Most of that outrageous spending is based on emotion anyway. If you meet your spouse's need in communication, then your wife or husband won't run out and purchase that car, television, diamond ring, expensive outfit, or yacht without first consulting with you.

If lack of finances was the main cause of marital failure, then why don't the members of the Amish communities, the Bruderhof communities, or the Anabaptists experience high rates of divorce? They certainly don't spend much money. They don't have a 401K or an IRA account, or stocks and bonds. All of the real estate is owned collectively by their communities. They don't have any personal wealth, yet couples stay together. Now, I am not saying that their lifestyle is either good or bad. I'm just pointing out that even in the absence of financial wealth, good communication can still keep a marriage going.

Let's look at the flip side. You can have as much money as Donald Trump and no communication, and the marriage will be on the rocks. Money simply helps you to purchase things that make your life easier and more comfortable. However, money cannot talk to you when you need some encouragement. Your spouse can, though. Yes, sex is good. But communication is better.

Get to know the person whom you are making love to. I promise you that it will strengthen your marriage far more than anything else will.

Chapter Nine

Five Things That Lead to the Death of a Marriage

Given enough time, each one of the things I mention here contains enough poison to kill a good marriage. I am listing only five (they are not in any order of importance); the list could be far more expansive. But throughout my years of counseling, these seem to be the five top reasons people throw in the towel. In many instances, one of these five things has been the impetus for committing far greater sins against the marriage vows. I fully believe that if you will avoid becoming victimized by any one of these listed "things to beware of," you will be on the road to creating a marriage that will last a lifetime as God intended.

#1 — ALLOWING YOUR PARENTS TO CONTROL YOUR MARRIAGE

Therefore shall a man leave his father and his mother, and shall cleave unto his wife: and they shall be one flesh (Genesis 2:24 KJV).

I have a pastor friend who, from the very start, allowed his mother to control his marriage. In fact, the very decision to get married was not his own but his mother's manipulative control over his life. He tells me that if he could do it again he would still marry the same woman, for he loves his wife dearly. However, he got married far too young.

He was not established nor was he ready to take on the major responsibilities that come with marriage and rearing a family. And his mother wanted to control every area of their lives from what they ate for dinner each day to what kind of furnishings went in their apartment to what style of clothes his wife wore. Needless to say, his wife did not welcome her involvement.

After two short years their marriage was so shaky that they teetered on the brink of divorce. The only way that my pastor friend felt he could save his marriage was to separate from his mother. It was a tough decision because the family ties were close, but he knew that he was making the right choice. Unfortunately, to this day his mother has an extreme dislike for her son's wife. She hates the fact that she no longer has control of their lives.

However, this couple now have been married more than ten years and are raising a beautiful family. Had my friend continued to allow his mother to rule their marriage, he would not have one.

Some people can't seem to break away from momma and daddy. If you can't break away, then it's better for you to stay single. Although this man's mother is not happy, it really does not matter. He has a responsibility to honor his mother, yes, but not to make her happy at the expense of his wife. He will always have a mother, but he might not always have had his new family had he ignored the obvious signs. Which relationship is worth more? You do the math.

#2 — RECEIVING UNGODLY COUNSEL

Blessed is the man who does not walk in the counsel of the wicked or stand in the way of sinners or sit in the seat of mockers (Psalm 1:1 NIV).

You need to be very careful about who you allow to give you advice concerning your marriage. Not everyone who offers advice is actually concerned about your best interest. Especially do not receive advice from unbelievers. They will give you advice based on their limited and sinful views of the world. Many non-Christians do not know that marriage is a godly institution. They take the wedding vows lightly, sort of like the rules for joining a fitness club.

Sister, don't talk to your girlfriend about your husband. Brother, don't talk to the guys about your wife. All that accomplishes is to give someone else the information he or she needs to do what you have not been doing and replace you. Don't even talk

Five Things That Lead to the Death of a Marriage

to family members about your spouse. Disgruntled siblings and parents can be just as destructive to your marriage as strangers can. If you have to release some steam, talk with a godly pastor. Even in that, I recommend that both married parties be present. Remember, there are always two sides to every story.

It is true that ministers of God are anointed to help save marriages, and many have done just that. But you, too, are anointed to help save your marriage. Talk to each other. You would be amazed at how your own advice could put things back together. If that doesn't work, talk to God. After all, He is the One who created marriage anyway. There is incredible power in prayer. But whatever you do, don't receive ungodly counsel.

#3 — LIVING AT HOME WITH PARENTS

For this reason a man shall leave his father and mother and be joined to his wife, and the two shall become one flesh (Matthew 19:5).

It is totally unacceptable to live at home with your parents after you are married. This is a major killer of marriages. It is no accident that God's Word declares you must leave your father and mother when you get married. This fundamental principle is crucial. Too many people disregard it in the name of convenience—to their detriment.

Every man needs his space. He needs a place where he can dominate his surroundings. If he does not have that, he will be more apt to give in to secret sinful tendencies as a release. He needs a place where his rules rule. It is close to impossible to live with your parents and make rules in their house. They're the ones who have always been the rulers and dominators of their household. Whether you like it or not, in their eyes you are somewhat of a subordinate. That viewpoint does not change just because you are married.

Every man needs his space.

A line of submission is always proper in a household. As long as you live in someone else's house, their household rules

— 143 —

reign. That is not the way for a newlywed couple to live. Perhaps you have heard the statement, "Two women can't live under the same roof." That is true. At some point your wife and your mother will knock heads in disagreement.

Agreement is the place of power, victory, and increase. Before agreement comes, though, sometimes there may be disagreement, differences in opinions, and ambivalence. The whole process, though it seems negative, has the potential to produce strength. But, when you live at home with your parents, you will not be able to go through the process with your wife. A parent will always feel somewhat obligated to choose the side of his or her child in a matter.

Their "choosing sides" will inevitably make you feel intruded upon and violated. Why? You need your space. You need the right atmosphere in which to nurture a healthy marital relationship. Also, you need to be allowed to fail in your attempt to properly communicate, yet get back up and try again. When you live at home with mom and dad, these options are not available to you.

I know the cost of living in some parts of the country may be sky-high. Perhaps you want to save for a down payment on a home of your own. Your parents' house is just a buffer, a temporary stopping place until you have enough money to make your move. Although that goal is a worthy one, it is still better for your marriage—in both the short and long run—if you get an inexpensive apartment. It doesn't matter what it looks like; it's yours. It is a place you can call home and have dominion in it. Whether it's an apartment, mobile home, or rented house, you need your own space in order to build the proper foundation for a marriage that will last. Friend, it's time to move out!

#4 — THE SPIRIT OF PRIDE

Pride goes before destruction, and a haughty spirit before a fall (Proverbs 16:18).

Nothing kills like pride. Pride is the original sin. It is this sin that caused Satan to get kicked out of heaven. It is the same sin that will destroy any marriage over a period a time. And it can attack anyone.

Pride, in short, *never* admits wrongdoing. In the marriage, pride creeps in when you or your spouse refuses to admit to a wrongdoing or shortcoming. It does not matter who you are. It does not matter how sweet, compassionate, and kind you are to your spouse. There will come a time when you will either do or say something that is totally wrong. No one is immune to this mistake. Never being wrong is not the problem. The real problem is when you are wrong but you refuse to confess that you are wrong. Such a recalcitrant spirit will inevitably destroy you.

Try it now. Can you say, "I was wrong, and I'm sorry"? There, you're still alive, aren't you? It was humbling, but it didn't hurt. I recommend that you repeat this statement each time you do something wrong toward your spouse.

Pride is a demonic spirit. The spirit of pride always usurps authority over God. Whether this spirit shows up in a choir director named Lucifer, a king called Nebuchadnezzer, or in you, it's still the same spirit.

It is this spirit that you must avoid at all cost. We all need the virtue of humility in many areas of our lives, but nowhere as much as in marriage. Face it, you can't always be right. Neither are you always wrong. Even a broken clock is right two times each day. Although it is right two times each day, it is wrong all the other times.

Maybe you are not in the wrong often. Maybe you're wrong only half the time. It doesn't matter. The point is, don't allow pride to stop you from enjoying a solid and healthy marriage. Your marriage is and always will be far more important than your desire to be right. And don't forget it!

#5 — PUTTING YOUR ULTIMATE TRUST IN MAN

Trust in the Lord with all your heart, and lean not on your own understanding; in all your ways acknowledge Him, and He shall direct your paths (Proverbs 3:5–6).

Although it is important for you to have a high level of trust in your spouse, you cannot depend on them for total trust. They are human, and humans fail. We have always been prone to failure, and we always will be. The only one you should ever put your total trust in is God. The reason is obvious. *God cannot fail.*

I am saddened when I see women and men so hurt by their spouses that they just can't do anything anymore. They become totally unproductive. Yes, what that spouse did might have been totally unacceptable. It might have been totally wrong. But that still is not a reason to totally shut down and be unfruitful.

I've seen both men and women worry themselves sick. Their worry so controls them that they refuse to eat anything and inevitably lose so much weight that it's unhealthy. I've seen some hire psychiatrists in the hopes that the doctor will solve their problems or at least give a logical reason why this offense happened to them. Others go so far as to take drugs (legal or illegal) in an attempt to escape from their pain.

The only one you should ever put your total trust in is God.

All such behavior is unacceptable in the sight of the Lord. Now, I am not justifying anyone's wrongdoing. Wrong is wrong. Sin is sin. There are obvious consequences for sin not repented of. My point is that such a response to that sin is unsatisfactory in God's eyes because it focuses more on the temporary problem rather than the permanent solution—God.

Yes, you should trust your husband or wife. But your ultimate trust should be put in God. Your spouse is only human. And when they do fall prey to that human nature, you might cry, be upset, and even be downright angry. God understands your response. However, God does not appreciate your quitting, caving in, giving up, and throwing in the towel.

When you do that, you are saying by your actions that your spouse has become your God! That is idolatry. Now, there is a fine line here. You must commit wholly to your spouse, yes. No one should be allowed to come between you and cause separation. However, you also have to choose loyalty to God above loyalty to any other person, even your spouse. The choice must always end with God. Put your total confidence in God, and everything else will fall into place. He has promised so.

Chapter Ten

God's Marriage—The Model for Success

Isn't it good to save the best for last? If you want to know how to have a lasting marriage, then the best example to model our marriages after is found in God's Word. It is God's covenant with Israel. Through it we clearly see the necessary characteristics of faithfulness, loyalty, perseverance, and most importantly, love and forgiveness. All throughout the Old Testament we see how God dealt with Israel—His chosen people and His bride.

GOD IS FAITHFUL NO MATTER WHAT

One thing you need to understand about God and marriage is that God's faithfulness is not predicated on the faithfulness of the one He is married to. In other words, God does not free Himself from His oath to be faithful just because we violated the covenant vow. He is faithful regardless of our behavior. That is a very difficult concept for most of us to comprehend since we predicate our faithfulness on the other person's reciprocating the same favor. The Word of God bears witness to God's faithfulness:

> *Blessed is he whose help is the God of Jacob, whose hope is in the Lord his God, the Maker of heaven and earth, the sea, and everything in them—the Lord, who remains **faithful forever*** (Psalm 146:5–6 NIV, emphasis added).

We live in a generation in which married couples divorce over the most inane things: stupid reoccurring arguments, lack of money, having too much money, weight gain, weight loss, and what we have come to call "irreconcilable differences." That term itself has been taken totally out of context. Not only that, but it also gives the average married person a legal right to break the bonds that God said are inseparable.

In this way we Christians have become much like the world. We think and behave as they do. I know this because God's actions are just the opposite of ours, especially as it relates to marriage. Even though Israel was an unfaithful bride, God continued to reach out to her. God continued to not only offer His forgiveness, but also make restitution with His bride. He continually offered a way to make things right.

People today operate just the opposite. They try to find reasons to quit and sever the relationship. Why? They do not have a faithful character. Please understand that faithfulness is a character issue, not a circumstantial issue. It's not something you do because the situation is to your liking. It is God's character to be faithful no matter what. He cannot be unfaithful. If He were to be unfaithful, He would not be God.

It is God's nature to commit forever. Be like Him. Perhaps you are experiencing some very disheartening situations in your marriage. A faithful character will find the solution to those situations every time. A faithful character seeks ways to make relationships work, not end. That is why it is so vitally important for you to know God. Every married couple should seek God. When you become like God, you possess His attributes—including faithfulness.

God's character is to be faithful no matter what.

Now, let me balance things out. I don't want you to run off with these statements and believe that I am advocating your staying in a relationship where you are being beat half to death by your spouse. That's a literal fulfillment of the "till death do us part" vows, and that's not the way to do it. Godly sense will tell you that such abuse is in direct opposition to a godly marriage.

If you are in such a situation, I pray you will immediately seek out professional and spiritual help. I simply want to impress the need for reinstating the lost value of permanence in marriage.

Just as God desires, I, too, desire you to get the vision of your marriage lasting throughout life's toughest storms. It is in the tough times that you become one.

> *For we are members of His body, of His flesh and of His bones. "For this reason a man shall leave his father and mother and be joined to his wife, and the two shall become one flesh." This is a great mystery, but I speak concerning Christ and the church. Nevertheless let each one of you in particular so love his own wife as himself, and let the wife see that she respects her husband* (Ephesians 5:30–33).

When we read this Scripture, we understand that it does not mean we literally become a part of Jesus' physical bone structure. Neither are our spouses expected to offer us their bones. No, this Scripture is simply conveying how faithfulness can make a relationship so strong that nothing in the world can divide it. It describes a fusing process in which two separate entities are joined together to become one.

It's sort of like welding two pieces of steel together. The two become one in the midst of the fire. Unlike glue, welding actually makes the steel stronger. When heated, glue loses its adhesive quality. Have you ever had your rearview mirror fall off on an extremely hot day? The mirror falls off because it is not one with the front window. It is merely glued on. To put it another way, the rearview mirror is not faithful to the front window. It will stick on only as long as the glue holds it together.

God expects the believer to act differently from the world when under the pressures of life's fires. When it gets hot, we are to get closer. No matter how difficult the times get, we become fused together. Although the church, as Christ's bride, does not always behave like she should, Christ's commitment to her grows stronger under fire and persecution. Why? Because God is faithful! Nothing less is expected from you.

I FORGIVE YOU

One of the most fundamental yet overlooked messages in the Scriptures is the message of forgiveness. Forgiveness is a key foundational block in building a strong marriage. I strongly suggest that everyone and anyone who provides premarital counseling services deal strongly with the area of forgiveness. It is vastly important. In fact, if you are not ready to forgive, then you are not ready to be married. If you are not ready to forgive, then you are not ready to live life to its fullest potential. Unforgiveness hinders growth and development.

A common misunderstanding about forgiveness says that when you forgive someone, you let that person off the hook. You think that person is now free from the consequences of his or her actions. Be honest. Doesn't that make you mad when you think that? Doesn't it make you so angry that you say in your heart, "That's not fair. I'm just not going to forgive them"? You tell yourself, "I'm not going to let them off the hook that easy. I refuse to forgive them."

If you are not ready to forgive, then you are not ready to be married.

What you fail to realize is that when you talk like that, you are only holding yourself hostage. You are only making your life that much more miserable and unproductive. In case you did not know, forgiveness does not free the other person. *Forgiveness frees you.* As I mentioned earlier, when we become more like Christ, we take on His nature. Not only is God faithful, but He also is forgiving.

Sometimes I am amazed at so-called saints who claim to have so much of God within them, yet who refuse to forgive another person. It is God's nature to forgive. It's built into His character. His forgiving nature is the main reason God does not harbor feelings of guilt, remorse, bondage, and vindictiveness. He chooses to forgive. And we are to be like Him!

Forgiveness actually frees you from the aftermath of the other person's bad choice. Can you imagine what life would be like if you chose to forgive and move on? What could your marriage be like if you did not harbor past issues in your heart? It is truly possible that you could have a marriage that is heaven on earth. But it requires forgiving first and asking questions later. Refusing to forgive only hinders the progress of your future. It also tips people off that you possess an ungodly spirit of arrogance.

You are not better than Jesus Christ. Let me clarify. The Bible tells us that prior to His crucifixion, some people treated Christ with horrible contempt. Some lied about Him; others physically and emotionally abused Him. They demeaned our Lord by spitting on Him, something that you would not even do to an animal. Yet, Jesus asked His Father to forgive His accusers. He told His Father that they did not understand what they were doing.

Could you, given those circumstances, forgive your enemies? Jesus did. I know that we all have a ways to go before we look just like Jesus. However, we are not exempt from the obligation to love each other so much that we forgive one another and move on. Thus forgiveness is absolutely crucial in marriage. I have seen so many couples split over issues that, if forgiven, would have provided a stronger base for marital growth.

Before you make the conscious decision not to forgive, first meditate on the words of our Lord Jesus just before He was crucified:

> Then Jesus said, "Father, forgive them, for they do not know what they do." And they divided His garments and cast lots (Luke 23:34).

LOVE COVERS SIN

> And above all things have fervent love for one another, for "love will cover a multitude of sins" (1 Peter 4:8).

Of all things to end this book on, I couldn't choose a better principle than this: Love covers sin.

God is and always will be our greatest example of a love relationship. Today the opposite of God's principles is commonplace. In our society, it seems like fidelity has become shameful and lewdness is rewarded. What a deep need America has for God's mercy and grace, wrapped in the package called love!

Although Israel continued to sin by whoring after other gods, God continued to love His people. God's plan and purpose remained in place because He already knew that we humans would fail. That is why God commissioned His Son to redeem us back to Him, paying the highest price possible: His life. There is no greater love than for One to offer His only Son as payment for sin.

> For God so loved the world that He gave His only begotten Son, that whoever believes in Him should not perish but have everlasting life. For God did not send His Son into the world to condemn the world, but that the world through Him might be saved (John 3:16–17).

> Greater love has no one than this, than to lay down one's life for his friends (John 15:13).

God shows us by His extreme example how *agape* love—unconditional love—has the power to overcome sin and ultimately conquer it. His expression of love can forgive us and release us from our sin. What would happen in your marriage if you followed this same example? Would it be just possible that your marriage would get stronger over time? Perhaps your passion for each other would grow immeasurably, just as God's love for us continues unabated.

Far too often people confuse trust with love. In the previous chapter I said you should put your ultimate trust only in the Lord. Nevertheless, people still put all their trust in humanity. What if your partner falls short of your expectations? Are you automatically shattered because you expected so much more of him or her? Perhaps you should be only upset, not shattered.

Here is the winning formula. Give *limited trust* and *unlimited love* for humankind. If you live by this formula, your heart won't break as often as it has. Why? Love covers all your sin and gives you another chance. Notice I did not say that love hides your sin. Everything that is hidden will come to the light.

When you truly love someone, your love forgives him or her, and that forgiveness then acts as if the event never happened. Just as faithfulness and forgiveness are both characteristics of God, so is love. God is love. He is not a portion of love; *He is totally love.* And I repeat, if we are to be more like Christ, then we must exercise more love. What better time and place to begin practicing unconditional love than in your marriage? Love your spouse no matter what.

God has been married a long time now. His bride hasn't always been perfect, but she will be someday. Meanwhile, His love continues to cover us. This is our example for a lasting, lifelong marriage. I know beyond any doubt that if you will follow His example of faithfulness, forgiveness, and love; if you will do what you need to before you say "I do," you too will enjoy marriage as God created it to be.

And now abide faith, hope, love, these three; but the greatest of these is love (1 Corinthians 13:13).

About the Author

Worshipper, entrepreneur, pastor, and pulpiteer extraordinaire, Stenneth E. Powell's preaching ministry has spanned the breadth and width of the United States of America for more than thirty years. Powell is a gifted orator who captivates audiences by articulating the truth of God in a way that is singularly unique. Through God's eyes Pastor Powell has been viewed in many capacities. Having an unquestionable apostolic mandate on his life, he planted churches both in Connecticut, his native home, and in Raleigh, North Carolina, his place of assignment. Having done no real research, geographical survey, or analysis of the area, Powell heeded the voice of the Lord to leave Connecticut and move to Raleigh, North Carolina, where he did not have any friends or family. Like Abraham, Brother Powell followed his spiritual impulse and uprooted his growing family to relocate to Raleigh at the Lord's command.

In May of 1990 he organized Abundant Life Christian Center with just six members. Today Pastor Powell ministers to more than 1500 parishioners each week. From its humble beginnings in a rented post office God has blessed the ministry now with its own 1000-seat sanctuary and a 24,000-square foot Family Life Center that includes a gymnasium, a complete fitness center, a full service computer lab, and a recording studio. Prior to his pastorate, he traveled for more than a decade as a National Evangelist for one of our nation's largest church organizations. As a seer, Pastor Powell always seeks out ways to build the lives of people. He envisions life for his parishioners as God's will originally intended it to be: *"Thy kingdom come. Thy will be done in earth, as it is in heaven"*

(Matthew 6:10 KJV). He serves on a number of ecumenical and faith-based organizations, some of which include the Fellowship of Inner City Word of Faith Churches headed by Dr. Frederick K.C. Price, the Raleigh Interdenominational Minister's Alliance, and the Advisory Board for the Pastors and Elders Council of the Church of God in Christ, which he chairs.

For as long a he could remember, Powell has had a knack for business and entrepreneurial exploits. This drive led him to spend years studying business at the University of Hartford. More recently, Powell launched a music publishing company whose principle goal is to help young gifted musicians, writers, and singers have an opportunity to launch a successful career in the arts. His greatest earthly achievement, though, is his bride of more than twenty-two years: Beverly Ann Powell. From this union, his pride continues through his two sons Stenneth Jr. and Joshua, both of whom are actively involved in their father's ministry.